SECOND EDITION

VOLUME SIX
Ferdinand Monjo to Chris Raschka

Favorite Children's AUTHORS *and* ILLUSTRATORS

E. Russell Primm III, Editor in Chief

PO Box 326, Chanhassen, MN 55317-0326
800/599-READ
http://www.childsworld.com

A Note to Our Readers:

The publication dates listed in each author's or illustrator's selected bibliography represent the date of first publication in the United States.

The editors have listed literary awards that were announced prior to August 2006.

Every effort has been made to contact copyright holders of material included in this reference work. If any errors or omissions have occurred, corrections will be made in future editions.

Photographs: 12—Annick Press; 16—Arthur Cohen Photography / Houghton Mifflin; 20, 24, 60, 100, 104, 140, 148, 152—Scholastic; 28—Katherine Lambert Photography; 32, 52, 112, 136—Simon & Schuster; 36—de Grummond Collection, University of Southern Mississippi; 40—C. Cady / Kerlan Collection, University of Minnesota; 44, 144—Harcourt; 48—Barry E. Levine / HarperCollins; 56—Houghton Mifflin; 64—Candlewick Press; 72—Plymouth Photo Studio / Houghton Mifflin; 80—Tom Bauer / Dorothy Hinshaw Patent; 84—Loomis Patterson / HarperCollins; 92, 120—Penguin Putnam; 96—North-South Books; 108, 132—HarperCollins; 116—Kathy McLaughlin; 128—Frederick Warne & Co. / Kerlan Collection, University of Minnesota.

An Editorial Directions book

Library of Congress Cataloging-in-Publication Data

Favorite children's authors and illustrators / E. Russell Primm III, editor-in-chief. — 2nd ed.
    v. cm.
  Includes bibliographical references and index.
  Contents: v. 1. Verna Aardema to Ashley Bryan.
  ISBN-13: 978-1-59187-057-9 (v.1 : alk. paper)
  ISBN-10: 1-59187-057-7 (v. 1 : alk. paper)
  ISBN-13: 978-1-59187-058-6 (v. 2 : alk. paper)
  ISBN-10: 1-59187-058-5 (v. 2 : alk. paper)
  ISBN-13: 978-1-59187-059-3 (v. 3 : alk. paper)
  ISBN-10: 1-59187-059-3 (v. 3 : alk. paper)
  ISBN-13: 978-1-59187-060-9 (v. 4 : alk. paper)
  ISBN-10: 1-59187-060-7 (v. 4 : alk. paper)
  ISBN-13: 978-1-59187-061-6 (v. 5 : alk. paper)
  ISBN-10: 1-59187-061-5 (v. 5 : alk. paper)
  ISBN-13: 978-1-59187-062-3 (v. 6 : alk. paper)
  ISBN-10: 1-59187-062-3 (v. 6 : alk. paper)
  ISBN-13: 978-1-59187-063-0 (v. 7 : alk. paper)
  ISBN-10: 1-59187-063-1 (v. 7 : alk. paper)
  ISBN-13: 978-1-59187-064-7 (v. 8 : alk. paper)
  ISBN-10: 1-59187-064-X (v. 8 : alk. paper)
  1. Children's literature—Bio-bibliography—Dictionaries—Juvenile literature. 2. Young adult literature Bio-bibliography—Dictionaries—Juvenile literature. 3. Illustrators—Biography—Dictionaries—Juvenile literature. 4. Children—Books and reading—Dictionaries—Juvenile literature. 5. Young Adults—Books and reading—Dictionaries—Juvenile literature. I. Primm, E. Russell, 1958–
  PN1009.A1F38 2007
  809'.8928203—dc22
  [B]   2006011358

TABLE OF CONTENTS

Major Children's Author and Illustrator Literary Awards

The American Book Awards

Awarded from 1980 to 1983 in place of the National Book Award to give national recognition to achievement in several categories of children's literature

The Boston Globe–Horn Book Awards

Established in 1967 by Horn Book *magazine and the* Boston Globe *newspaper to honor the year's best fiction, poetry, nonfiction, and picture books for children*

The Caldecott Medal

Established in 1938 and presented by the Association for Library Service to Children division of the American Library Association to illustrators for the most distinguished picture book for children from the preceding year

The Carnegie Medal

Established in 1936 and presented by the British Library Association for an outstanding book for children written in English

The Carter G. Woodson Book Awards

Established in 1974 and presented by the National Council for the Social Studies for the most distinguished social science books appropriate for young readers that depict ethnicity in the United States

The Coretta Scott King Awards

Established in 1970 in connection with the American Library Association to honor African American authors and illustrators whose books are deemed outstanding, educational, and inspirational

The Hans Christian Andersen Medal

Established in 1956 by the International Board on Books for Young People to honor an author or illustrator, living at the time of nomination, whose complete works have made a lasting contribution to children's literature

THE KATE GREENAWAY MEDAL
Established by the Youth Libraries Group of the British Library Association in 1956 to honor illustrators of children's books published in the United Kingdom

THE LAURA INGALLS WILDER AWARD
Established by the Association for Library Service to Children division of the American Library Association in 1954 to honor an author or illustrator whose books, published in the United States, have made a substantial and lasting contribution to children's literature

THE MICHAEL L. PRINTZ AWARD
Established by the Young Adult Library Services division of the American Library Association in 2000 to honor literary excellence in young adult literature (fiction, nonfiction, poetry, or anthology)

THE NATIONAL BOOK AWARDS
Established in 1950 to give national recognition to achievement in fiction, nonfiction, poetry, and young people's literature

THE NEWBERY MEDAL
Established in 1922 and presented by the Association for Library Service to Children division of the American Library Association for the most distinguished contribution to children's literature in the preceding year

THE ORBIS PICTUS AWARD FOR OUTSTANDING NONFICTION
Established in 1990 by the National Council of Teachers of English to honor an outstanding informational book published in the preceding year

THE PURA BELPRÉ AWARD
Established in 1996 and cosponsored by the Association for Library Service to Children division of the American Library Association and the National Association to Promote Library Services to the Spanish Speaking to recognize a writer and illustrator of Latino or Latina background whose works affirm and celebrate the Latino experience

THE SCOTT O'DELL AWARD
Established in 1982 and presented by the O'Dell Award Committee to an American author who writes an outstanding tale of historical fiction for children or young adults that takes place in the New World

Ferdinand Monjo

Born: August 28, 1924
Died: October 9, 1978

I

t's no wonder that Ferdinand Monjo loved writing about history.
His own family had an adventurous past, and many of his relatives were involved in historical events. Monjo wanted to show kids how
exciting history really was. That's what inspired him to write children's
books about historical people and events.

Ferdinand Nicholas Monjo III was born in Stamford, Connecticut,
in 1924. His father's family had its origins in Spain. Once they arrived
in the United States, they went into the fur-trading business. Relatives
told Ferdinand about the family's trading ships that sailed to Alaska to
trade with the Inuit for furs. Ferdinand's mother's family came from
Mississippi. Her relatives told him tales about plantation life and the
Civil War (1861–1865).

These firsthand accounts made an impression on Ferdinand. He
realized that history could be much more thrilling than dry facts and
dates. He later recalled: "Hearing my two families discuss the past—

MONJO WAS WORKING ON A BOOK CALLED *THREE KINDS OF SCARED* AT THE TIME
OF HIS DEATH. HIS SON JUSTIN COMPLETED IT, AND IT WAS PUBLISHED IN 2001.

often with considerable heat and color—made it clear to me that people like [General Ulysses S.] Grant and [President Abraham] Lincoln certainly had been flesh-and-blood creatures."

After attending Stamford High School, Monjo enrolled in New York City's Columbia University, graduating in 1946. In 1950, he married Louise Elaine Lyczak. Over the years, they had three sons and a daughter.

Soon, Monjo began a career as a children's book editor at several New York City publishing companies. From 1953 to 1958, he was the editor of Golden Books at Simon and Schuster. Next, he became the editor of the *American Heritage Junior Library* at American Heritage Press. In 1961, he moved to Harper and Row, where he was the assistant director of children's books. Then in 1969, he became vice president and editorial director of children's books at Coward, McCann and Geoghegan. He remained in this position until he died.

While working as an editor, Monjo began to feel that children's history books were not very entertaining. The problem, he concluded,

"We need to inspire our gifted young people to make an attempt at greatness. . . . I want my books to incite children to dare to do something marvelous. For, if they dare, perhaps they will succeed."

WHEN HE WROTE, MONJO USED THE NAME F. N. MONJO.

F. N. MONJO

Poor Richard in France

pictures by
BRINTON TURKLE

A Selected Bibliography of Monjo's Work

Three Kinds of Scared (with Justin Monjo, 2001)

A Namesake for Nathan: Being an Account of Captain Nathan Hale by His Twelve-Year-Old Sister (1977)

Gettysburg: Tad Lincoln's Story (1976)

Letters to Horseface (1975)

Grand Papa and Ellen Aroon (1974)

The Sea-Beggar's Son (1974)

Poor Richard in France (1973)

The Vicksburg Veteran (1971)

The Drinking Gourd (1970)

Indian Summer (1968)

was that they left out the kind of details that really made history fun. He was determined to fill this gap by writing history books himself.

Monjo's first book, *Indian Summer*, was published in 1968. It tells about a pioneer family in Kentucky that fends off an attack by Native Americans. His next book, *The Drinking Gourd*, tells the dramatic story of African American slaves who escaped to freedom before the Civil War.

In his biographies of famous people, Monjo wanted children to see how human his subjects were. He made sure to tell about their flaws, mistakes, and foolish moments. He felt this would enable readers to perceive historical figures as realistic, understandable human beings.

Monjo often explored history through a child's eyes. *Poor Richard in France* tells about Benjamin Franklin from his grandson's point of view. Monjo used this same concept in *Grand Papa and Ellen Aroon*. It portrays President Thomas Jefferson through the eyes of his granddaughter.

However he approached his subjects, Monjo shared his passion for history with young readers. He died in New York City in 1978 at the age of fifty-four.

> *"This is what I feel I can do: give a child his first authentic taste of a great figure from the past."*

WHERE TO FIND OUT MORE ABOUT FERDINAND MONJO

BOOK
Berger, Laura Standley, ed. *Twentieth-Century Children's Writers.* 4th ed. Detroit: St. James Press, 1995.

WEB SITE
CHILDREN'S LITERATURE NETWORK
http://www.childrensliteraturenetwork.org/brthpage/08aug/8-28monjo.html
For a brief biography of the author

THE TITLE OF MONJO'S *THE DRINKING GOURD* REFERS TO THE GROUP OF STARS KNOWN AS THE BIG DIPPER. RUNAWAY SLAVES USED IT AS A SORT OF MAP THAT POINTED THEIR WAY TO FREEDOM IN THE NORTH.

Robert Munsch

Born: June 11, 1945

R obert Munsch is a born storyteller. He has written more than forty children's books. But he's especially good at telling stories aloud, in person. For decades, he's been a popular storyteller at daycare centers, libraries, and schools.

Robert Norman Munsch was born in 1945 in Pittsburgh, Pennsylvania. He grew up as the fourth child in a family of nine children. When

he was little, Robert loved books by Dr. Seuss. His very favorite was *The Five Hundred Hats of Bartholomew Cubbins.* He did poorly in elementary school, although he did enjoy writing poetry.

In high school, Robert decided he wanted to become a Roman Catholic priest. So he spent seven years studying for the priesthood. In 1969, he received

MUNSCH IS CANADA'S BEST-SELLING AUTHOR OF CHILDREN'S BOOKS.

a history degree from Fordham University in New York City. Then he went to Boston, Massachusetts, where he earned a master's degree in anthropology from Boston University in 1971.

During his studies, Munsch took a part-time job in a day-care center. There he found that he had a natural gift for making up stories to tell the kids. Munsch's experience as a storyteller changed his career plans. He decided to switch his studies to childhood education. As he recalled, "I liked the kids better than anthropology."

Munsch then enrolled at Tufts University in Massachusetts, earning a master's degree in child studies in 1973. That same year, he married Ann

A Selected Bibliography of Munsch's Work

I'm So Embarrassed! (2006)

Smelly Socks (2004)

Andrew's Loose Tooth (1998)

Alligator Baby (1997)

Where Is Gah-Ning? (1994)

I Have to Go! (1987)

Love You Forever (1986)

Thomas's Snowsuit (1985)

Mortimer (1983)

The Boy in the Drawer (1982)

Murmel, Murmel, Murmel (1982)

Jonathan Cleaned Up, Then He Heard a Sound; or, Blackberry Subway Jam (1981)

The Paper Bag Princess (1980)

The Dark (1979)

The Mud Puddle (1979)

> *"My stories all develop through storytelling to groups of children. My goal when I make them up is to keep an audience happy."*

Beeler. Their family eventually grew to include three children—Julie, Andrew, and Tyya. The newlyweds moved to Coos Bay, Oregon, where Munsch worked as a teacher at Bay Area Childcare.

In 1975, the Munsches settled in Guelph, in the Canadian province of Ontario. There Munsch worked at the University of Guelph as an assistant professor and also the head teacher at the university's Family Studies Laboratory Preschool. Again, he entertained the preschoolers with his stories.

Eventually, Munsch began writing some of his stories down and submitting them to publishers. In 1979, *The Mud Puddle* and *The Dark* became his first published books. In *The Mud Puddle*, a little girl contends with a pesky puddle. That same girl vanquishes a monster in *The Dark*. The first story Munsch had ever told, *Mortimer*, became a book in 1983.

Munsch's characters are often gutsy, high-spirited kids who solve their problems in silly, magical, or imaginative ways. Many of his stories involve repetition, making it easy for kids to join in and repeat the words. But *Love You Forever* is a bit different. It's a much more thoughtful tale, treating issues of aging parents and death.

MANY OF MUNSCH'S BOOKS ARE ILLUSTRATED BY MICHAEL MARTCHENKO. THE FIRST OF THESE WAS *THE PAPER BAG PRINCESS*, PUBLISHED IN 1980.

Munsch sometimes spends as much as three years telling his stories to live audiences to make sure they work when presented aloud. Only then does he write them down and send them to a publisher.

> *"Most books I have written have been inspired by one particular child and his or her experience."*

Munsch is still writing books at home in Guelph. He also makes recordings in which he narrates his children's stories. But his favorite way to tell stories is still in person, with a roomful of kids gathered around him.

∾

WHERE TO FIND OUT MORE ABOUT ROBERT MUNSCH

BOOKS

Berger, Laura Standley, ed. *Twentieth-Century Children's Writers.* 4th ed. Detroit: St. James Press, 1995.

Rockman, Connie C., ed. *Eighth Book of Junior Authors & Illustrators.* New York: H. W. Wilson, 2000.

WEB SITES

LIFE AND TIMES
http://www.cbc.ca/lifeandtimes/munsch.html
To see excerpts from a documentary about Robert Munsch

ROBERT MUNSCH
http://www.robertmunsch.com/
For a biography, photos of Robert Munsch, and information about visits, what's new, and his books and poems

———

MUNSCH'S STORY *JONATHAN CLEANED UP, THEN HE HEARD A SOUND; OR, BLACKBERRY SUBWAY JAM* WAS RELEASED AS AN ANIMATED FILM BY THE NATIONAL FILM BOARD OF CANADA IN 1984.

Jim Murphy

Born: September 25, 1947

Whether he writes about wars, wolf packs, or disasters, Jim Murphy serves up spellbinding stories for young readers. Murphy started out as an ordinary kid who became a manual laborer and an editor. Now he is the author of more than twenty books for children and young adults.

Jim Murphy was born in 1947 in Newark, New Jersey. He grew up in nearby Kearny, a middle-class suburb with quiet, tree-lined streets. Jim and his friends played ball and shared typical boyhood adventures. They imagined they were explorers as they tramped along the Passaic River. Pretending they were soldiers, they scouted out old factory buildings for "enemies."

Jim was a poor student in grammar school. In seventh grade, however, he developed a passion for history. In his high school, Saint

MURPHY IS MARRIED TO ALISON BLANK. THEY HAVE TWO SONS—MICHAEL AND BEN.

Benedict's Preparatory School in Newark, Jim excelled at track. He was on his school's national championship track team, and he was one of the nation's top-ten high school sprinters.

Jim wasn't much of a reader—until he was forbidden to read something, that is. One of his teachers forbade the students to read Ernest Hemingway's *A Farewell to Arms*. The teacher felt the adult content of this war story made it unsuitable for young readers. Jim immediately read the book and anything else he thought his teacher might disapprove of. He also began to dabble at writing himself.

Jim Murphy was not a total bookworm, though. He had great mechanical skills, and he held some interesting side jobs in his late teens and early twenties. He repaired boilers, tarred roofs, put up fences, and worked as a metalworker on construction projects.

In 1970, Murphy earned a degree from Rutgers University in New Brunswick, New Jersey. That same year, he went to work at Seabury Press in New York City. (Seabury later became Clarion Books.) During his seven years there, Murphy moved up from editorial secretary to managing editor. He also began to try his hand at writing children's books. In 1977, on his thirtieth birthday,

> *"Children weren't just observers of our history. They were actual participants and sometimes did amazing and heroic things."*

MURPHY LOVES TO COOK. HE MAKES EAST INDIAN, FRENCH, AND CHINESE FOODS, AS WELL AS PIZZA.

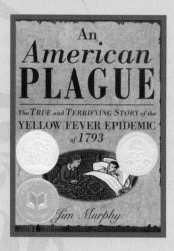

A Selected Bibliography of Murphy's Work

Murphy's Major Literary Awards

2004 Newbery Honor Book
2004 Boston Globe–Horn Book Nonfiction Award
2004 Orbus Pictus Award
   An American Plague: The True and Terrifying Story of the Yellow Fever Epidemic of 1793

1996 Orbus Pictus Award
1995 Boston Globe–Horn Book Nonfiction Honor Book
1994 Newbery Honor Book
   The Great Fire

1994 Orbis Pictus Award
   Across America on an Emigrant Train

he decided to quit his job and concentrate on writing.

In his early books, Murphy brings his mechanical interests into play. His first book, *Weird and Wacky Inventions*, came out in 1978. It describes odd contraptions that people have invented over the years. Murphy went on to write several animal books. *Dinosaur for a Day* and *The Last Dinosaur* are told from the dinosaurs' viewpoint. *The Call of the Wolves* recounts a wolf's harrowing experiences after getting separated from its pack.

Murphy became best known, however, for his historical books. In *The Great Fire*, he tells about the enormous

> *"I'd helped a number of writers come up with ideas, helped them focus their texts and in some cases even rewritten them. So why not try to do it for myself, I thought."*

Chicago fire in 1871 through the eyes of people who survived it. *The Boys' War: Confederate and Union Soldiers Talk about the Civil War* and *The Long Road to Gettysburg* focus on the Civil War (1861–1865). They tell the personal stories of ordinary young soldiers.

Immigrant life, disease outbreaks, and the environment are some other subjects that Murphy covers with gripping realism and sensitive insights. He still works at his home in Upper Montclair, New Jersey.

ॐ

WHERE TO FIND OUT MORE ABOUT JIM MURPHY

BOOK
Holtze, Sally Holmes, ed. *Seventh Book of Junior Authors and Illustrators.* New York: H. W. Wilson, 1996.

WEB SITES
CBC MAGAZINE
http://www.cbcbooks.org/cbcmagazine/meet/jim_murphy.html
To read a short biography and the author's words about his writing

JIM MURPHY
http://www.jimmurphybooks.com/
For a biography, information about the author's books, and current news

LEARNING ABOUT JIM MURPHY
http://www.scils.rutgers.edu/~kvander/murphy.html
To read an autobiographical excerpt

———

MURPHY READS MORE THAN FOUR HUNDRED BOOKS A YEAR.

Christopher Myers

Born: October 17, 1974

Christopher Myers got his start by working with a collaborator—the famous African American poet and writer Walter Dean Myers. Walter is Christopher's father. The two produced several books together, but really the partnership began much earlier.

"My father was always working on something which he would ask me to research, mostly African American and labor history," Christopher Myers explains. "For example, my uncle worked in the coal mines of West Virginia. There was an accident. He would have died in the mine shaft had not a woman come by and heard his cries for help. She stayed with him for three days in the mine shaft

CHRISTOPHER MYERS AND HIS FATHER, WALTER DEAN MYERS, WORKED ON *HARLEM: A POEM* SEPARATELY, EACH PURSUING HIS OWN IDEAS. "WE'VE GOT DIFFERENT VISIONS," CHRISTOPHER EXPLAINS.

until he got better. Later she became my aunt."

Christopher Myers was born in New York City on October 17, 1974, and has been drawing since he was a child. In fact, he enrolled at an art school at the age of thirteen.

For college, he attended Brown University in Providence, Rhode Island. Myers majored in American history and art semiotics—the study of how images create meaning. After graduation, Myers took part in the American Art Independent Studio Program, a special program for artists run by the Whitney Museum in New York.

Because his father writes children's books, Myers had long been thinking about them.

A Selected Bibliography of Myers's Work

A Time to Love: Tales from the Old Testament (Illustrations only, 2002)

Blues Journey (2002)

Fly (2001)

Wings (2000)

Black Cat (1999)

Monster (Illustrations only, 1999)

This I Know: Poetry across Black Cultures (Illustrations only, 1998)

Harlem: A Poem (Illustrations only, 1997)

Galápagos: Islands of Change (1995)

Shadow of the Red Moon (Illustrations only, 1995)

Forest of the Clouded Leopard (Text only, 1994)

Turnip Soup (Text only, 1994)

McCrephy's Field (Text only, 1991)

Myers's Major Literary Awards

2003 Boston Globe-Horn Book Picture Book Honor Book
    Blues Journey

2000 Coretta Scott King Illustrator Honor Book
    Black Cat

1999 Boston Globe-Horn Book Fiction Honor Book
    Monster

1998 Caldecott Honor Book
1998 Coretta Scott King Illustrator Honor Book
1997 Boston Globe-Horn Book Fiction Honor Book
    Harlem: A Poem

> *"Every time my family gets together, it's Harlem that's on their minds. . . . Harlem is a very different place now . . . but it's still the place that has formed a lot of who I am. I see ways now that . . . Harlem is a legacy, Harlem is an attitude."*

He felt that many children's books talked down to young readers. He wanted to change that. He also felt that African Americans needed to see images and pictures that related to them.

Myers's first illustration project was for his father's science fiction book *Shadow of the Red Moon,* which was published in 1995. The two also worked together on *Harlem: A Poem,* a picture book published in 1997. It was based on his father's poetic tribute to the neighborhood where he grew up.

Harlem, in New York City, has been the center of black culture in the United States for generations. It is also an important part of the family history of many African Americans.

Myers used collage to illustrate his father's poem. He says that the technique, which involves cutting out images and

> *"Illustrating children's books is a trip. So many people are starving for images. Image famine in African America. I think we are learning how important images are, how much they do."*

IN HIS ART, MYERS LIKES TO MAKE COLLAGES USING AFRICAN AMERICAN MAGAZINES SUCH AS *EBONY, ESSENCE,* AND *VIBE.*

pasting them together, has connections with African American art forms such as jazz, blues, and quilting.

Myers has also written and illustrated picture books of his own. The best-known is *Wings.* It tells the story of a boy who is teased by the other kids at school because he can fly. Myers has also illustrated a collection of poems by African Americans.

In addition to working on his books, Christopher A. Myers is an artist, a children's photographer, and a clothing designer. He lives in Brooklyn, New York.

ᐳᐸ

WHERE TO FIND OUT MORE ABOUT CHRISTOPHER MYERS

BOOKS

Rockman, Connie C., ed. *The Ninth Book of Junior Authors and Illustrators.*
New York: H. W. Wilson Company, 2004.

Silvey, Anita, ed. *The Essential Guide to Children's Books and Their Creators.*
Boston: Houghton Mifflin Company, 2002.

WEB SITE

SCHOLASTIC KIDS FUN ONLINE
http://books.scholastic.com/teachers/authorsandbooks/authorstudies/authorhome.jsp?
authorID=2369&collateralID=5249&displayName=Biography/
To read an autobiographical sketch of Christopher A. Myers

THE MAIN CHARACTER IN *WINGS* IS IKARUS JACKSON.
THE NAME COMES FROM THE GREEK MYTH OF ICARUS, WHO BUILT
A PAIR OF WINGS AND ESCAPED FROM AN ISLAND PRISON.

Walter Dean Myers

Born: August 12, 1937

Sometimes the barriers we face in life lead us in directions we hadn't previously considered. For Walter Dean Myers, a speech impediment led him to the world of books. Books, in turn, inspired his writing career.

Walter Dean Myers was born on August 12, 1937, in Martinsburg, West Virginia. When Walter was two, his mother died. His father was very poor and had several children. The Dean family in New York City, who were friends of Walter's mother, offered to take in young Walter. His father agreed to send Walter to live with them.

The Dean family lived in Harlem, the largest African American neighborhood in the United States. Growing up there gave Walter a child's perspective of African American culture. He played basketball and stickball until it was too dark to see. He listened to the many languages spoken in

---

FOR FUN, MYERS ENJOYS PLAYING THE FLUTE, DOING CROSSWORD PUZZLES, AND CHASING HIS CAT, ASKIA, AROUND THE HOUSE.

the neighborhood. He went to plays at nearby Columbia University, to church services, to Bible school, and to story readings at the public library.

Once Walter learned to read, he read everything he could get his hands on—from comic books to magazines and newspapers. A teacher brought him a stack of books one day from her own personal library. They opened up a whole new world for Walter.

> *"Books took me, not so much to foreign lands and fanciful adventures, but to a place within myself that I have been exploring ever since."*

Walter was a good student and could read very well, but a speech difficulty made it hard for him to communicate. He often retreated into books to escape this hardship. A teacher suggested writing down his thoughts and ideas as a way to overcome the problem.

Soon, Walter was writing poems and short stories. By high school, Walter had discovered what he called his "avenue of value"—his way of finding self-esteem through his writing.

Because his family could not afford college, Walter Dean Myers left high school at the age of sixteen and spent three years in the army. Then he held various jobs, including loading trucks and working at the post office, but he never stopped writing.

Myers wrote at night after work. He was soon writing magazine pieces and advertising copy. When he saw that the Council on Interracial

---

MYERS WAKES BETWEEN 4:30 AND 5:00 A.M. AND
WALKS FIVE MILES WEARING A WEIGHTED VEST.

A Selected Bibliography of Myers's Work

Jazz (2006)

Blues Journey (2002)

145th Street: Short Stories (2000)

At Her Majesty's Request: An African Princess in Victorian England (1999)

Monster (1999)

Harlem: A Poem (1997)

Slam! (1996)

Malcolm X: By Any Means Necessary (1993)

Somewhere in the Darkness (1992)

Now Is Your Time! The African American Struggle for Freedom (1991)

Fallen Angels (1988)

Scorpions (1988)

Motown and Didi: A Love Story (1984)

Where Does the Day Go? (1969)

Myers's Major Literary Awards

2003 Boston Globe–Horn Book Picture Book Honor Book
Blues Journey

2000 Boston Globe–Horn Book Fiction Honor Book
145th Street: Short Stories

2000 Coretta Scott King Author Honor Book
2000 Michael L. Printz Award
1999 Boston Globe–Horn Book Fiction Honor Book
Monster

2000 Orbis Pictus Honor Book
At Her Majesty's Request: An African Princess in Victorian England

1997 Boston Globe–Horn Book Fiction Honor Book
Harlem: A Poem

1997 Coretta Scott King Author Award
Slam!

1994 Coretta Scott King Author Honor Book
Macolm X: By Any Means Necessary

1993 Coretta Scott King Author Honor Book
1993 Newbery Honor Book
1992 Boston Globe–Horn Book Fiction Honor Book
Somewhere in the Darkness

1992 Carter G. Woodson Outstanding Merit Book
1992 Coretta Scott King Author Award
1992 Orbis Pictus Honor Book
Now Is Your Time! The African American Struggle for Freedom

1989 Coretta Scott King Author Award
Fallen Angels

1989 Newbery Honor Book
Scorpions

1985 Coretta Scott King Author Award
Motown and Didi: A Love Story

1980 Coretta Scott King Author Award
The Young Landlords

Books for Children was holding a contest for black writers of children's books, he created *Where Does the Day Go?* He won, and the story became his first published book.

When Myers showed an editor a short story he had written about teenagers, the editor asked for the rest of the book. *Fast Sam, Cool Clyde, and Stuff* became Myers's first young-adult novel.

During his career, Myers has written picture books, middle-grade books, science fiction, fantasy, nonfiction, and mystery-adventure stories. He has touched on many important issues, such as suicide, teen pregnancy, adoption, and parental neglect. He has also worked with his son, writer and illustrator Christopher A. Myers.

Myers talks about growing closer to his characters as he works on a book, so that his readers can grow close to them as well. Many readers feel as though the characters in his books quickly become old friends.

> *"Writing for me has been many things. It was a way to overcome the hindrance of speech problems. . . . It was a way of establishing my humanity in a world that often ignores . . . those in less favored positions."*

WHERE TO FIND OUT MORE ABOUT WALTER DEAN MYERS

BOOKS

Jones, Lynda. *Five Famous Writers.* New York: Scholastic, 2001.

Jordan, Denise. *Walter Dean Myers: Writer for Real Teens.* Springfield, N.J.: Enslow, 1999.

Myers, Walter Dean. *Bad Boy: A Memoir.* New York: HarperCollins, 2001.

WEB SITES

EDUCATIONAL PAPERBACK ASSOCIATION
http://edupaperback.org/showauth.cfm?authid=63
To read an autobiographical sketch of and a booklist for Walter Dean Myers

TEENREADS.COM
http://www.teenreads.com/authors/au-myers-walterdean.asp
For biographical information about the author

———

MYERS BEGINS EACH NEW BOOK WITH AN OUTLINE.
HE THEN CUTS OUT PICTURES OF ALL OF THE CHARACTERS
FOR A COLLAGE THAT HE PLACES ON THE WALL ABOVE HIS COMPUTER.

Phyllis Reynolds Naylor

Born: January 4, 1933

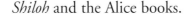

R eading and telling stories have always been an important part of Phyllis Reynolds Naylor's life. She has written more than one hundred books for both adults and children, and she has won many awards for her children's books. Her best-known children's books include *Shiloh* and the Alice books.

Phyllis Reynolds Naylor was born on January 4, 1933, in Anderson, Indiana. Her father was a traveling salesman, so the family moved many times. During the summers, her family would go to either Iowa or Maryland to visit her grandparents. These experiences became a big part of the books that Naylor would later write.

Phyllis grew up during the Great Depression. Her family did not have much money,

---

NAYLOR DOESN'T USE OUTLINES WHEN SHE WRITES. SHE FINDS THEM "LIMITING."

but there were always good books to read. "My mother, and sometimes my father, read aloud to us every night," Naylor remembers. Her father even imitated characters while he read the stories. Storytelling is something she always remembers from her childhood.

As a young girl, Phyllis could hardly wait until she learned how to read and write. By the time she was in the fifth grade, writing was her favorite hobby. She would rush home from school each day to write a story. When Phyllis was sixteen years old, she had her first story published, in a church magazine.

After high school, Naylor went to college and studied to become a clinical psychologist.

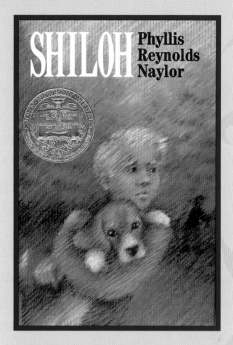

A Selected Bibliography of Naylor's Work

Alice in Know (2006)
Anyone Can Eat Squid (2005)
Girls Rule! (2004)
Bernie Magruder and the Bats in the Belfry (2003)
Blizzard's Wake (2002)
The Boys Return (2001)
Carlotta's Kittens and the Club of Mysteries (2000)
Alice on the Outside (1999)
Achingly Alice (1998)
"I Can't Take You Anywhere!" (1997)
Alice in April (1993)
Shiloh (1991)
Bernie and the Bessledorf Ghost (1990)
The Witch's Eye (1990)
One of the Third-Grade Thonkers (1988)
Beetles, Lightly Toasted (1987)
The Keeper (1986)
How I Came to Be a Writer (1978)
Witch's Sister (1975)
To Make a Wee Moon (1969)
The Galloping Goat and Other Stories (1965)

Naylor's Major Literary Awards

1992 Newbery Medal
  Shiloh

> *"And so, because I want to know what it would be like to be a preacher or a bicycle courier or a motherless twelve-year-old or a bridge worker, I write."*

As a student, she wrote stories and sold them to help pay for her college tuition. When she received her degree, Naylor decided that she wanted to be a writer. Since that time, she has been writing for both children and adults.

In her books for young people, Naylor is known for her ability to write from a young person's point of view. She writes both fiction and nonfiction books. Her books cover a wide range of topics. Her books have included advice on how to maintain friendships and ways to communicate with family members. Naylor's fiction books have explored many difficult issues that young people face today.

She has always written for both adults and young people. "I can never imagine myself writing only for children or only for adults," Naylor notes. "I like to follow up a mystery story for the nine-to-twelve set with a contemporary novel for adults. After

> *"Whatever you have felt or seen or heard or done or even thought about doing—no matter how brave, how cowardly, how disgusting, or how adventurous—someone else has thought of too. When you put your thoughts and feelings down on paper, you can trust your readers to understand."*

SOME OF NAYLOR'S HOBBIES ARE HIKING, BIKING, SINGING, AND GOING TO THE THEATER.

that perhaps I will do a picture book or a realistic novel for teens, or possibly a humorous book for children."

Naylor lives in Bethesda, Maryland, with her husband and two cats. She continues to write for both adults and children. Naylor says, "On my deathbed, I am sure, I will gasp, 'But I still have five more books to write!' "

⌒

WHERE TO FIND OUT MORE ABOUT PHYLLIS REYNOLDS NAYLOR

BOOKS

Hill, Christine M. *Ten Terrific Authors for Teens.*
Berkeley Heights, N.J.: Enslow, 2000.

Kovacs, Deborah, and James Preller. *Meet the Authors and Illustrators: 60 Creators of Favorite Children's Books Talk about Their Work.* Vol. 2. New York: Scholastic, 1993.

Naylor, Phyllis Reynolds. *How I Came to Be a Writer.*
New York: Atheneum, 1978.

Nuwer, Hank. *To the Young Writer: Nine Writers Talk about Their Craft.* Danbury, Conn.: Franklin Watts, 2002.

WEB SITES

EDUCATIONAL PAPERBACK ASSOCIATION
http://edupaperback.org/showauth.cfm?authid=64
To read an autobiographical sketch of and a booklist for Phyllis Reynolds Naylor

INTERNET PUBLIC LIBRARY
http://www.ipl.org/div/kidspace/askauthor/Naylor.html
To read an autobiographical sketch of and an interview with Phyllis Reynolds Naylor

———

SHILOH IS BASED ON THE TRUE STORY OF A STRAY DOG NAYLOR
FOUND WHEN VISITING THE TOWN OF SHILOH, WEST VIRGINIA.

Kadir Nelson

Born: May 15, 1974

Kadir Nelson's paintings appear in art galleries around the world. His art is known for its striking detail, graceful lines, and emotional energy. Fortunately for children, Nelson has also used his gifts to illustrate more than a dozen picture books for kids.

Kadir Nelson was born in Washington, D.C., in 1974 and spent his early years in Atlantic City, New Jersey. He began drawing when he was three years old. As a child, Kadir's favorite books were *Where the Wild Things Are* and *In the Night Kitchen* by Maurice Sendak. His favorite subjects in school were math and art.

Kadir's mother moved the family to San Diego, California, in 1983. When Kadir was eleven, he spent the summer in Maryland with his uncle

---

IN HIS ILLUSTRATIONS, NELSON OFTEN USES A COMBINATION OF PENCIL, OIL PAINTS, AND WATERCOLORS.

Mike. That uncle was artist Michael Morris, who began teaching Kadir how to further his artistic abilities.

While attending San Diego's Crawford High School, Kadir started entering his paintings in art competitions. Eventually, he won a scholarship to study art at the Pratt Institute in Brooklyn, New York. After graduation in 1996, he got married. He also began getting offers for work.

"I'd like to encourage children to follow their dreams and work hard to make them come true. And, oh, make something beautiful!"

First, *Sports Illustrated* magazine asked Nelson to illustrate a football story. That was the first time his artwork was published. At the same time, DreamWorks movie studio asked him to create illustrations that were used to develop the movie *Amistad*. This movie tells the heroic story of captives who took control of the slave ship *Amistad* in 1839.

"The best thing about doing children's books is that I get to relive my childhood."

Nelson's first illustrated book—*Brothers of the Knight* by Debbie Allen—was published in 1999. It puts a modern spin on an old fairy tale, placing the story's action in the African American community of Harlem in New York

---

AS A CHILD, KADIR ENJOYED COMIC BOOKS AND COMIC STRIPS. HIS FAVORITE ILLUSTRATOR WAS CHARLES SCHULZ, WHO CREATED THE *PEANUTS* COMIC STRIP.

A Selected Bibliography of Nelson's Work

Michael's Golden Rules (Illustrations only, 2006)

He's Got the Whole World in His Hands (2005)

Please, Puppy, Please (Illustrations only, 2005)

Ellington Was Not a Street (Illustrations only, 2004)

Thunder Rose (Illustrations only, 2003)

Please, Baby, Please (Illustrations only, 2002)

Under the Christmas Tree (Illustrations only, 2002)

The Village That Vanished (Illustrations only, 2002)

Just the Two of Us (Illustrations only, 2001)

Salt in His Shoes: Michael Jordan in Pursuit of a Dream (Illustrations only, 2000)

Brothers of the Knight (Illustrations only, 1999)

Nelson's Major Literary Awards

2005 Coretta Scott King Illustrator Award
   Ellington Was Not a Street

2004 Coretta Scott King Illustrator Honor Book
   Thunder Rose

City. Through his illustrations, Nelson conveys the energetic spirit of twelve brothers who dance their shoes into rags every night.

Nelson's illustrations add a heartwarming touch to *Just the Two of Us*. This book explores the relationship between a father and his son from the child's birth to adulthood. The text of the book comes from actor Will Smith's hit song "Just the Two of Us."

Nelson's radiant paintings portray the warmth of a loving home in *Under the Christmas Tree*, a collection of holiday poems by Nikki Grimes.

Nelson explores a serious African theme in *The Village*

That Vanished by Ann Grifalconi. It's about an African village that escaped a raid by slave traders. In *Ellington Was Not a Street* by Ntozake Shange, he portrays many African American artists and writers of the 1940s.

In 2005, Nelson decided to showcase a traditional African American spiritual song. In *He's Got the Whole World in His Hands,* the artist uses pencils, oils, and watercolors to convey the warmth of God's love.

Kadir Nelson lives in San Diego, California, with his wife and two daughters.

⁂

WHERE TO FIND OUT MORE ABOUT KADIR NELSON

BOOKS

Rockman, Connie C., ed. *The Ninth Book of Junior Authors and Illustrators.*
New York: H. W. Wilson Company, 2004.

Sutherland, Zena. *Children and Books.* 9th ed. Boston: Allyn & Bacon, 1997.

WEB SITES

THE COLLECTION SHOP
http://www.thecollectionshop.com/Kadir_Nelson_Art_Collection.asp
To read a biography of Kadir Nelson

G.R.I.T.S. KIDZ BOOK CLUB
http://www.gritskidz.com/Interviews/ill_nelson.html
For an interview with the artist

KADIR NELSON HOME PAGE
http://www.kadirnelson.com/
For a biography, his art, his books, and what's new

NELSON'S ILLUSTRATIONS HAVE APPEARED IN *SPORTS ILLUSTRATED* AND THE *NEW YORKER* AS WELL AS IN THE *NEW YORK TIMES.*

Evaline Ness

Born: April 24, 1911
Died: August 12, 1986

A t first, Evaline Ness planned to become a librarian. Instead she worked as a fashion illustrator for many years. Then at last, she found her true calling as an illustrator of children's books.

She was born Evaline Michelow in Union City, Ohio, in 1911, and grew up in Pontiac, Michigan. As a child, Evaline loved art. When her sister wrote stories about knights and princesses, Evaline illustrated them with pictures she cut out from magazines. In school, her attempts at art were not appreciated. She submitted drawings for her high school yearbook, but they were rejected.

In 1931, she enrolled in Ball State Teachers College in Muncie, Indiana, to study library science. For an English class assignment, she painted a series of pictures illustrating King Arthur's court. They were on display in the classroom for a whole week. This reawakened the

---

NESS STUDIED ART AT THE ACCADEMIA DE BELLE ARTI, A DISTINGUISHED ART SCHOOL IN ROME, ITALY, FROM 1951 TO 1952.

young woman's desire to be an artist. The next year, she transferred to the School of the Art Institute of Chicago. During her two years of study there, she also worked as a fashion artist and magazine illustrator.

In 1938, she married Eliot Ness, the legendary crime fighter portrayed in the TV series *The Untouchables*. The couple made their home in Cleveland, Ohio, where Evaline worked as a fashion illustrator for a department store. In 1942, they moved to Washington, D.C. Eliot took a job with the U.S. government, while Evaline studied at the Corcoran School of Art.

As Eliot's work occupied more and more of his time,

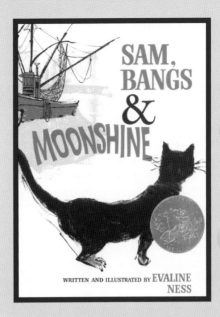

WRITTEN AND ILLUSTRATED BY EVALINE NESS

A Selected Bibliography of Ness's Work

A Hand-Me-Down Doll (Illustrations only, 1983)

A Victorian Paper House: To Cut Out and Color (1978)

Paper Palace: To Cut Out and Color (1976)

Yeck Eck (1974)

Old Mother Hubbard and Her Dog (Illustrations only, 1972)

Mr. Miacca: An English Folk Tale (Illustrations only, 1967)

Sam, Bangs and Moonshine (1966)

Tom Tit Tot: An English Folk Tale (Illustrations only, 1965)

A Pocketful of Cricket (Illustrations only, 1964)

All in the Morning Early (Illustrations only, 1963)

Josefina February (1963)

The Princess and the Lion (Illustrations only, 1963)

Thistle and Thyme: Tales and Legends from Scotland (Illustrations only, 1962)

The Sherwood Ring (Illustrations only, 1958)

The Bridge (Illustrations only, 1957)

The Story of Ophelia (Illustrations only, 1954)

Ness's Major Literary Awards

1967 Caldecott Medal
  Sam, Bangs and Moonshine

1966 Caldecott Honor Book
  Tom Tit Tot: An English Folk Tale

1965 Caldecott Honor Book
  A Pocketful of Cricket

1964 Caldecott Honor Book
  All in the Morning Early

> "*I really cannot tell you* **how** *I wrote* [Sam, Bangs and Moonshine]. All I know is that I sat at the typewriter for four days and nothing happened. On the fifth day it struck.*"

Evaline dreamed of pursuing her art career more seriously. The Nesses divorced in 1946, and Evaline moved to New York City. There she worked as a fashion illustrator for Saks Fifth Avenue department store.

In 1954, Ness illustrated her first children's book—*The Story of Ophelia* by Mary Gibbons. Next, she illustrated *The Bridge* by Charlton Ogburn. Soon she was hooked on children's book illustration. She quit her job at Saks in 1959 and married engineer Arnold Bayard that same year. Then she proceeded to create art for dozens of books.

Ness used many different techniques in her work. Because her pictures were printed on a flat page, she tried hard to give them texture and depth. She sometimes used woodcuts, cutting the design into blocks of wood that become the printing surface. She also used silk screening, a kind of stencil technique. Ness also created effects with ink splattering and even spitting!

Ness illustrated many books of fairy tales and folktales by other authors. *Josefina February*

> "*. . . I accepted almost every manuscript sent to me by publishers. Each one was a new exciting experience.*"

NESS LIVED ON THE CARIBBEAN ISLAND OF HAITI FOR A YEAR IN THE EARLY 1960S. THAT INSPIRED HER TO WRITE *JOSEFINA FEBRUARY*, WHICH TAKES PLACE IN HAITI.

was the first book that she both wrote and illustrated. It's the tale of a little girl and her baby burro. Another work she wrote and illustrated was *Sam, Bangs and Moonshine*. It's the story of a fisherman's daughter who tells too many lies. Ness also created cutout books. They featured buildings of different periods, such as *A Victorian Paper House: To Cut Out and Color*.

Evaline Ness died at the age of seventy-five in Kingston, New York.

❧

WHERE TO FIND OUT MORE ABOUT EVALINE NESS

BOOKS

Chevalier, Tracy, ed. *Twentieth-Century Children's Writers*. 3rd ed. Detroit: St. James Press, 1989.

Silvey, Anita, ed. *The Essential Guide to Children's Books and Their Creators*. Boston: Houghton Mifflin Company, 2002.

WEB SITES

BOOK HELP WEB
http://www.bookhelpweb.com/authors/nesse/ness.htm
For a biography of Evaline Ness

ENCYCLOPAEDIA BRITANNICA
http://www.britannica.com/ebi/article-9331182
For a biography and a review of her books

NESS TAUGHT CHILDREN'S ART CLASSES AT CORCORAN SCHOOL OF ART IN WASHINGTON, D.C., AND AT PARSONS SCHOOL OF DESIGN IN NEW YORK CITY.

Joan Lowery Nixon

Born: February 3, 1927
Died: June 28, 2003

Joan Lowery Nixon loved her high school English teacher. The teacher recognized Joan's talent for writing. She encouraged Joan to major in journalism in college. Nixon studied to be a journalist, but later she discovered her love for writing children's books. Joan Lowery Nixon wrote children's books for almost forty years. Her best-known books include *The Kidnapping of Christina Lattimore, The Mysterious Red Tape Gang, The Dark and Deadly Pool,* and *The Other Side of Dark.*

Joan Lowery was born on February 3, 1927, in Los Angeles, California. She lived in a large house with her parents and grandparents. Joan knew at an early age that she wanted to be a writer. She learned

---

NIXON GREW UP NEAR HOLLYWOOD, CALIFORNIA. SHE WOULD OFTEN
SEE MOVIE STARS AND OTHER FAMOUS PEOPLE IN HER NEIGHBORHOOD.

how to read when she was three years old and memorized words from her favorite books. She also asked her mother to write down poems for her.

> *"Journalism taught me to focus because I had to sit down and write, whether I felt like it or not—no waiting for inspiration. I learned the skill of finding the important facts in a story, and how to isolate them from all of the unnecessary details."*

In elementary school, Joan discovered her talent for story-telling. Her sisters and other kids from the neighborhood would gather in the family's playroom. They would ask Joan to tell them a story or perform a play. With her mother's help, Joan wrote scripts for puppet shows. She also told stories using the dolls from her dollhouse.

Joan was always writing stories when she was a young girl. She even had a poem published in a children's magazine when she was ten years old. She became more interested in writing in junior high school, and she became the editor of the school newspaper.

After high school, she attended the University of Southern California. She met Hershell Nixon at the university. They married in 1949. After college, Joan Lowery Nixon could not find a job in journalism. Instead, she took a teaching job in Los Angeles.

AFTER HER FIRST BOOK WAS PUBLISHED, NIXON TAUGHT WRITING AT SCHOOLS, LIBRARIES, AND COLLEGES. SHE ALSO WROTE A HUMOR COLUMN FOR A DAILY NEWSPAPER IN HOUSTON, TEXAS.

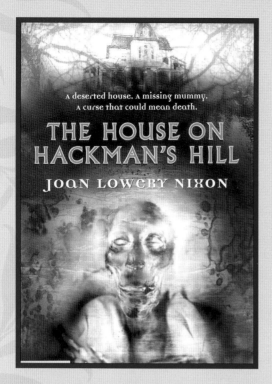

A Selected Bibliography of Nixon's Work

The Making of a Writer (2002)

The Trap (2002)

Gus and Gertie and the Lucky Charms (2001)

Ann's Story, 1747 (2000)

The Haunting (2000)

Aggie's Home (1998)

Circle of Love (1997)

Beware the Pirate Ghost (1996)

Land of Hope (1992)

The Weekend Was Murder! (1992)

Whispers from the Dead (1989)

The Dark and Deadly Pool (1987)

A Family Apart (1987)

Fat Chance, Claude (1987)

Haunted Island (1987)

Beats Me, Claude (1986)

The Other Side of Dark (1986)

The House on Hackman's Hill (1985)

The Stalker (1985)

The Séance (1980)

The Kidnapping of Christina Lattimore (1979)

The Mysterious Red Tape Gang (1974)

Mystery of Hurricane Castle (1964)

In the following years, Nixon and her husband moved several times throughout the country. By the time they moved to Texas, Nixon was the mother of four children. She was still interested in writing, but she did not have much time to do it.

While living in Texas, Nixon saw a notice for a writer's conference. She went to the conference and became excited about writing children's books. She worked for several years to write a book. When she finished the book, it was rejected by twelve publishers. Her first book, *Mystery of Hurricane Castle,* was finally published in 1964.

Nixon wrote more than 110 books for children and young people. She won many awards for her work, including three Edgar Allan Poe Awards.

Nixon continued to write mysteries as well as fiction and nonfiction books for children and young people until her death in 2003.

"I'm more challenged when I write for young people because when you write for 'children' you write for everyone from a two-year-old to a teenager. There are so many, many different styles and forms for these age groups."

WHERE TO FIND OUT MORE ABOUT JOAN LOWERY NIXON

BOOKS

Kovacs, Deborah, and James Preller. *Meet the Authors and Illustrators: 60 Creators of Favorite Children's Books Talk about Their Work.* Vol. 2. New York: Scholastic, 1993.

Nixon, Joan Lowery. *The Making of a Writer.*
New York: Delacorte Press, 2002.

WEB SITES

SCHOLASTIC
http://teacher.scholastic.com/writewit/mystery/index.htm
To read mystery writing tips from Joan Lowery Nixon

TEENREADS.COM
http://www.teenreads.com/authors/au-nixon-joan-lowery.asp
To read a biographical sketch of Joan Lowery Nixon

NIXON ENJOYS INCLUDING "RED HERRINGS" IN HER MYSTERIES. THESE ARE BITS OF INFORMATION THAT ARE INTENDED TO MAKE HER READERS SUSPECT THE WRONG PERSON!

Mary Norton

Born: December 10, 1903
Died: August 29, 1992

Everyone knows the Borrowers. Pod and Homily Clock and their daughter Arrietty may be only six inches tall, but they are giants in children's books. They became instantly popular when Mary Norton introduced them in *The Borrowers* in 1953. Four more books followed. Radio programs, television shows, and movies were made about the Clock family. Children everywhere loved learning about these tiny imaginary people, who lived by "borrowing" the small items "human beans" lost every day.

Mary Norton thought up the idea of the Borrowers when she was a child. She was born Mary Spenser on December 10, 1903, in London, England. She spent most of her childhood in the small country town of Leighton Buzzard.

On walks with her four brothers, Mary would lag behind, daydreaming. What would it be like

THE BORROWER BOOKS WERE INSPIRED BY NORTON'S POOR EYESIGHT. SHE CAREFULLY STUDIED THE SMALL THINGS SHE COULD BRING CLOSE TO HER FACE, GIVING HER THE IDEA OF A TINY FAMILY WHO ALSO NOTICED TINY THINGS.

to walk through this field of tangled grasses and thorn bushes if you were only six inches tall? How would you get through the gates that human children climb over so easily?

Mary had imagined the Borrowers when she was very young. But she didn't write about them until much later. When she grew up, her first love was the theater. She became an actress at the Old Vic Theatre in London. Then she married Robert Norton and moved to his home in Portugal. Mary and Robert Norton had four children—Ann, Robert, Guy, and Caroline.

Mary Norton's life was turned upside down when World War II (1939–1945) broke out. She and the children

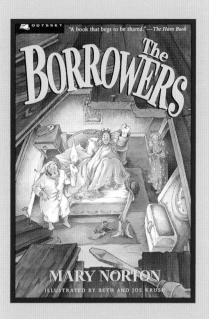

A Selected Bibliography of Norton's Work

The Borrowers Avenged (1982)
Are All the Giants Dead? (1975)
Poor Stainless: A New Story about the Borrowers (1971)
The Borrowers Aloft (1961)
The Borrowers Afloat (1959)
Bed-Knob and Broomstick (1957)
The Borrowers Afield (1955)
The Borrowers (1953)

Norton's Major Literary Awards

1952 Carnegie Medal
   The Borrowers

moved to England, then to the United States, and then back to England. She did war work to help support the family. And then she began writing books.

Norton's first two books were about an apprentice witch, Miss Price, and the three children she makes friends with. *The Magic Bed-Knob; or, How to Become a Witch in Ten Easy Lessons* and *Bonfires and Broomsticks* later combined into one book called *Bed-Knob and Broomstick*. The books were very popular and were made into both a radio program and a Walt Disney movie.

> *"I work terribly hard and sometimes rewrite a sentence six times over until the emphasis is on the right words and it falls in an interesting way. As long as one word sticks out like a sore thumb, I work on it until it reads so easily that nobody thinks I've worked so hard."*

When *The Borrowers* was published in 1953, though, Norton really became famous. Everyone loved the Borrowers— and reading about the dangers they faced from the humans who lived so close. Pod was brave, resourceful, and just a bit overprotective; Homily was loving but easily flustered; young Arrietty had a "questing spirit" that sometimes got her in trouble. You can learn a lot about life in England by reading the Borrower books. You can also learn a lot about what it means to be a human being—whether you are six inches tall or six feet tall.

———

NORTON ADORED BEING AN ACTRESS. SHE DESCRIBED HER YEARS AT THE OLD VIC THEATRE IN LONDON AS THE MOST MEMORABLE OF HER LIFE.

Mary Norton died in her home in Devonshire, England, on August 29, 1992. She was eighty-eight.

❧

WHERE TO FIND OUT MORE ABOUT MARY NORTON

BOOKS

McElmeel, Sharron L. *100 Most Popular Children's Authors: Biographical Sketches and Bibliographies.* Englewood, Colo.: Libraries Unlimited, 1999.

Silvey, Anita, ed. *The Essential Guide to Children's Books and Their Creators.* Boston: Houghton Mifflin Company, 2002.

WEB SITES

EASY FUN SCHOOL—THE BORROWERS
http://easyfunschool.com/article2083.html
For a literature unit on *The Borrowers* with suggested questions and activities

MARY NORTON
http://www.leighton-linslade.org.uk/Mary%20Norton/biog.htm
To read biographical information about Mary Norton

THE SF SITE FEATURED REVIEW: THE BORROWERS
http://www.sfsite.com/09b/bor41.htm
For reviews of Mary Norton's books and information about the author

———

NORTON PROBABLY DREW ON PERSONAL EXPERIENCE WHEN SHE WROTE *THE MAGIC BED-KNOB,* IN WHICH THREE CHILDREN LEAVE LONDON FOR THE COUNTRY DURING WORLD WAR II. SHE AND HER CHILDREN MOVED OFTEN TO ESCAPE THE BOMBING.

Laura Joffe Numeroff

Born: July 14, 1953

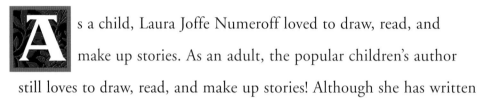

As a child, Laura Joffe Numeroff loved to draw, read, and make up stories. As an adult, the popular children's author still loves to draw, read, and make up stories! Although she has written more than thirty books, *If You Give a Mouse a Cookie* continues to be one of her readers' favorites.

Laura Joffe Numeroff was born on July 14, 1953, in Brooklyn, New York. Her father was an artist, and her mother was a teacher. "They both enriched my life with the love of reading, playing the piano, singing, dancing,

NUMEROFF OFTEN VISITS LIBRARIES AND BOOKSTORES. SHE ALSO COLLECTS CHILDREN'S BOOKS.

science, and stamp collecting." Laura was the youngest of three girls. She has two older sisters, Emily and Alice.

Laura's favorite childhood possessions were her microscope, a box of sixty-four crayons, and her library card. She loved to read. She would check out as many books at

> *"The best reviews come from kids who write me— that makes it all worth it!"*

one time as the library would let her have. She also loved to draw. Soon she was making up her own stories and drawing the pictures to go with them. She knew she wanted to be a writer.

In high school, Laura decided to be a fashion designer like her older sister Emily. She went to the Pratt Institute in New York City to study fashion design. Unfortunately, she discovered that she didn't like fashion design!

While she was in college, Numeroff took a course in writing and illustrating books for children. During the course, she wrote a story for one of her assignments. The story was called *Amy for Short*. This became Numeroff's first published book. Numeroff forgot all about fashion design. She was going to write and illustrate children's books.

Numeroff writes about everyday things and ordinary kids. Some of her stories are silly. That's one of the reasons children enjoy them.

NUMEROFF HAS HAD JOBS RUNNING A MERRY-GO-ROUND
AND WORKING AS A PRIVATE INVESTIGATOR.

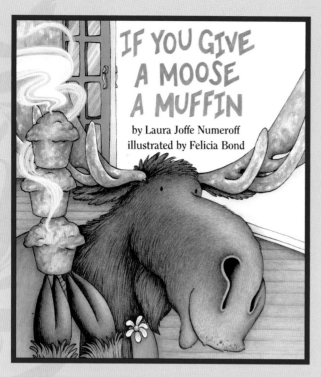

IF YOU GIVE A MOOSE A MUFFIN

by Laura Joffe Numeroff
illustrated by Felicia Bond

A Selected Bibliography of Numeroff's Work

When Sheep Sleep (2006)

If You Give a Pig a Party (2005)

Beatrice Doesn't Want To (2004)

Sherman Crunchley (2003)

Laura Numeroff's 10-Step Guide to Living with Your Monster (2002)

If You Take a Mouse to School (2000)

The Best Mouse Cookie (1999)

If You Give a Pig a Pancake (1998)

Sometimes I Wonder if Poodles Like Noodles (1998)

What Daddies Do Best (1998)

What Mommies Do Best (1998)

The Chicken Sisters (1997)

Two for Stew (1996)

Why a Disguise? (1996)

Chimps Don't Wear Glasses (1995)

Dogs Don't Wear Sneakers (1993)

If You Give a Moose a Muffin (1991)

If You Give a Mouse a Cookie (1985)

Amy for Short (1976)

When she writes, she's affected by her own reading taste. "I prefer biographies, nonfiction and stories dealing with 'real-life' dramas—[I] never did like fairy tales all that much. I guess that's why my children's stories tend to be based on things kids actually go through, like wearing braces, being too tall for your age, being a daydreamer, having to wear something your grandmother gave you even though you think it's hideous," says Numeroff.

As a child, Laura Joffe Numeroff dreamed of becoming a writer, and that dream has come true. "I'll always have a first love for children's books. I hope to be writing until my last days," says Numeroff.

❦

WHERE TO FIND OUT MORE ABOUT LAURA JOFFE NUMEROFF

BOOKS

Holtze, Sally Holmes, ed. *Seventh Book of Junior Authors & Illustrators.* New York: H. W. Wilson Company, 1996.

Major Authors and Illustrators for Children and Young Adults. Detroit: Gale Group, 2002.

WEB SITES

HOUGHTON MIFFLIN
http://www.eduplace.com/kids/hmr/mtai/numeroff.html
To read more about Laura Joffe Numeroff

KIDSREADS.COM
http://www.kidsreads.com/series/series-mouse-author.asp
To read an autobiographical sketch of Laura Joffe Numeroff

LAURA NUMEROFF'S HOME PAGE
http://www.lauranumeroff.com/
To read a biography and other information about Laura Joffe Numeroff

―――

NUMEROFF ENJOYED BEING A GIRL SCOUT, ESPECIALLY SELLING GIRL SCOUT COOKIES. THIN MINTS ARE STILL HER FAVORITE!

Robert C. O'Brien

Born: January 11, 1918
Died: March 5, 1973

The author of one of the most beloved children's books of all time, *Mrs. Frisby and the Rats of NIMH,* did not start writing fiction until the last ten years of his life. Writing under the pen name Robert C. O'Brien, the man born Robert Leslie Conly worked as a magazine editor, and wrote news stories, articles, and poetry for many years, but he saved his best work—his fiction—for last.

Robert Leslie Conly was born on January 11, 1918, in Brooklyn, New York. Robert was the third of five children in a literate, quick-

witted, sharp-tongued Irish family. More shy and withdrawn than his siblings, Robert often retreated into the fantasy world of his own imagination. There, he invented stories, starring himself as a hero.

Robert's parents were schoolteachers, and his father later worked as a reporter for the *New York Herald Tribune.* Growing up, Robert was surrounded by books,

O'BRIEN'S DAUGHTER, NOVELIST JANE LESLIE CONLY, WROTE TWO SEQUELS TO *MRS. FRISBY AND THE RATS OF NIMH: RACSO AND THE RATS OF NIMH* (1986) AND *R-T, MARGARET, AND THE RATS OF NIMH* (1990).

newspapers, and magazines. Reading soon became one of his great loves.

When he was an infant, Robert's family moved to Amityville, New York. Robert was smart and showed musical talent, but he was also anxious and often sick. He didn't like school, and he didn't always get along with his brothers and sisters. In many ways, he had a difficult and lonely childhood.

By the time he entered high school, Robert began to emerge from his shell. Noted for his quick wit, his singing and piano playing, and his excellent grades, Robert enjoyed his high school years.

Conly started college in 1935 at Williams College in

A Selected Bibliography of O'Brien's Work

Z for Zachariah (Completed by Conly's wife and daughter, 1974)
Mrs. Frisby and the Rats of NIMH (1971)
The Silver Crown (1968)

O'Brien's Major Literary Awards

1972 Newbery Medal
1971 Boston Globe-Horn Book Fiction Honor Book
   Mrs. Frisby and the Rats of NIMH

western Massachusetts, but the stress of being away from home got to him, and he dropped out during his sophomore year. After studying music and taking a few courses in New York City, Conly returned to college and got his bachelor's degree in English from the University of Rochester in Upstate New York.

After graduation, Conly took a job at an advertising agency and then went to work for *Newsweek* magazine. This marked the beginning of his successful career as a writer and editor. He married Sally McCaslin in 1943, and the couple moved to Washington, D.C. In that city, Conly worked for several newspapers before landing a job at *National Geographic* magazine, where he worked for the rest of his life.

> *"Since I am in the writing business, when I get a story idea I write it down before I forget it. It isn't always for children, but those are the stories I most like to write."*

Eventually, Conly and his family moved out of the city. They bought a farm within commuting distance of Washington. When eye problems forced Conly to move back to the city, he used the extra time to pursue his lifelong dream of writing fiction.

In 1968, Conly's first novel for children, *The Silver Crown,* was published under the pen name Robert C. O'Brien. That title was followed in 1971 by his award-winning *Mrs. Frisby and the Rats of NIMH.* In 1972, he

O'BRIEN LIVED ON A FARM. HIS FAVORITE PET WAS A SPARROW NAMED JENNY.

published a thriller for adults called *A Report from Group 17.*

Robert Leslie Conly, known to the world as Robert C. O'Brien, died on March 5, 1973, of a heart attack. He was only fifty-five. His final novel, *Z for Zachariah,* was completed by his daughter and his wife, and published after his death.

> *"Children like a straightforward, honest plot with a beginning, a middle, and an end: a problem, an attempt to solve it, and at the end a success or a failure."*

"[His readers] write him many letters—smudged, misspelled, tremendously moving documents," Conly's wife once said. "A surprising number begin, 'Dear Mr. O'Brien, I too am writing a book.' These letters he considers extra sacred. They are . . . from the special children, from the dreamers . . . from our future writers."

❧

WHERE TO FIND OUT MORE ABOUT ROBERT C. O'BRIEN

BOOK
De Montreville, Doris, and Elizabeth D. Crawford, eds. *Fourth Book of Junior Authors & Illustrators.* New York: H. W. Wilson Company, 1978.

WEB SITE
CENTER FOR CHILDREN'S BOOKS
http://bccb.lis.uiuc.edu/0204focus.html
To learn about Robert C. O'Brien's life and work

—

O'BRIEN CHOSE TO WRITE HIS NOVELS UNDER A PEN NAME. IT WASN'T UNTIL HIS DEATH THAT HE WAS REVEALED AS ROBERT LESLIE CONLY, AN EDITOR AT *NATIONAL GEOGRAPHIC* MAGAZINE.

Scott O'Dell

Born: May 23, 1898
Died: October 15, 1989

cott O'Dell had many different jobs before becoming a children's book author. He was a journalist, a cameraperson for movie studios, and a book editor. He also wrote many fiction and nonfiction books for adults. Later, O'Dell became an award-winning children's author. His best-known children's books include *Island of the Blue Dolphins, The King's Fifth, The Black Pearl,* and *Sing Down the Moon.*

Scott O'Dell was born on May 23, 1898, in Los Angeles, California. Scott and his family moved several times throughout southern California when he was a boy. He spent time exploring caves near the ocean and searching for fish and other animals.

TWO OF O'DELL'S CHILDREN'S BOOKS, *ISLAND OF THE BLUE DOLPHINS* AND *THE BLACK PEARL,* WERE ADAPTED INTO FILMS.

He grew to love the outdoors. This love for nature and the outdoors was often a theme in his children's books.

After graduating from high school, O'Dell attended four colleges. He never graduated from college. He only took classes that interested him and helped him with his writing.

When he left college, O'Dell joined a movie production crew. He worked as a camera operator on the filming of a movie in Italy. O'Dell wrote his first novel for adults while he was working on the movie. He also had several other jobs in the movie industry before becoming a full-time writer in 1934.

When O'Dell returned to the United States, he worked as a journalist, a columnist, and an editor. He also served as the book editor for a Los Angeles newspaper. During this time, he wrote several fiction and nonfiction books for adults. O'Dell wrote adult books for twenty-six years before publishing his first children's book in 1960.

> *"History has a very valid connection with what we are now. Many of my books are set in the past but the problems of isolation, moral decisions, greed, and the need for love and affection are problems of today as well."*

Island of the Blue Dolphins was O'Dell's first book for young people. He got the idea for the story while doing research for another book.

BEFORE BECOMING A WRITER, O'DELL WORKED ON A FARM.

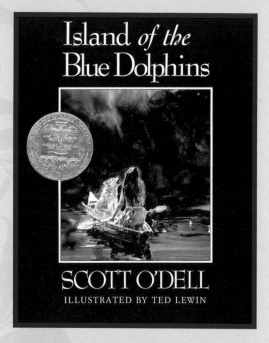

A Selected Bibliography of O'Dell's Work

My Name Is Not Angelica (1989)

Black Star, Bright Dawn (1988)

The Serpent Never Sleeps: A Novel of Jamestown and Pocahontas (1987)

Streams to the River, River to the Sea: A Novel of Sacagawea (1986)

Zia (1976)

The Hawk That Dare Not Hunt by Day (1975)

Child of Fire (1974)

Sing Down the Moon (1970)

The Black Pearl (1967)

The King's Fifth (1966)

Island of the Blue Dolphins (1960)

O'Dell's Major Literary Awards

1987 Scott O'Dell Award
   Streams to the River, River to the Sea: A Novel of Sacagawea

1972 Hans Christian Andersen Medal for Authors

1971 Newbery Honor Book
   Sing Down the Moon

1968 Newbery Honor Book
   The Black Pearl

1967 Newbery Honor Book
   The King's Fifth

1961 Newbery Medal
   Island of the Blue Dolphins

He found a newspaper article about a young girl who spent eighteen years on an island off the California coast. O'Dell was interested in this story and decided to write a book based on this young girl. When it was published, *Island of the Blue Dolphins* received many awards, including the Newbery Medal. The book continues to be popular among young readers.

Most of O'Dell's books for children are historical fiction. He used this format to help

"I do want to teach through books. Not heavy-handedly, but to provide a moral back-drop for readers to make their own decisions."

convey important messages to his readers. O'Dell used the themes of racial conflict, greed, and dealing with enemies in all of his books. Characters in his books also show great appreciation for animals, oceans, and the environment.

Scott O'Dell died on October 15, 1989, in Mount Kisco, New York. His last book for young people, *My Name Is Not Angelica,* was published the year of his death.

❧

WHERE TO FIND OUT MORE ABOUT SCOTT O'DELL

BOOKS

Kovacs, Deborah, and James Preller. *Meet the Authors and Illustrators: 60 Creators of Favorite Children's Books Talk about Their Work.* Vol. 1. New York: Scholastic, 1991.

McElmeel, Sharron L. *The 100 Most Popular Children's Authors: Biographical Sketches and Bibliographies.* Englewood, Colo.: Libraries Unlimited, 1999.

Russell, David L. *Scott O'Dell.* New York: Twayne Publishers, 1999.

WEB SITES

EDUCATIONAL PAPERBACK ASSOCIATION
http://edupaperback.org/showauth.cfm?authid=65
To learn more about Scott O'Dell's life and work

SCOTT O'DELL HOME PAGE
http://www.scottodell.com
For answers to frequently asked questions about O'Dell and information about the Scott O'Dell Award

---

IN 1982, O'DELL ESTABLISHED A BOOK AWARD FOR AUTHORS OF HISTORICAL FICTION FOR YOUNG PEOPLE. IT IS CALLED THE SCOTT O'DELL AWARD.

Mary Pope Osborne

Born: May 20, 1949

Because her father was in the army, Mary Pope Osborne moved many times when she was growing up. She had lived in Austria and in many different states by the time she was fifteen years old. She loved the adventure of moving and living in a new place. This thrill of adventure and travel is something she uses in her books. Osborne has been writing novels, picture books, and nonfiction books for children and young people for more than twenty years. She is best known for her Magic Tree House series of books.

Mary Pope Osborne was born on May 20, 1949, in Fort Sill, Oklahoma. She had a very close relationship with her parents, brothers, and sisters. This closeness made it easier when they moved to a new city. She loved to see new things when her family moved. She remembers a castle that was near their house in Austria and an old fort in Virginia. These and other

OSBORNE WAS ELECTED PRESIDENT OF THE AUTHOR'S GUILD IN 1993. THIS IS THE OLDEST ORGANIZATION OF PROFESSIONAL WRITERS IN THE UNITED STATES.

memories are part of the books she writes.

Her father retired from the army when Mary was a teenager, and the family moved to a small town in North Carolina. Mary missed the adventure of moving to different cities. She became involved in a community theater group where she found great adventure again. She worked both backstage and as an actor, performing many different roles in drama productions.

Next, she went on to study drama at the University of North Carolina. When she finished college, she traveled with a group of people throughout Asia. It was an exciting but dangerous trip. She got very sick, spent two weeks in

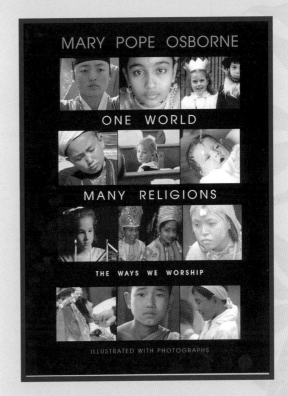

A Selected Bibliography of Osborne's Work

Blizzard of the Blue Moon (2006)

Carnival at Candlelight (2005)

Summer of the Sea Serpent (2004)

Haunted Castle on Hallows Eve (2003)

Good Morning, Gorillas (2002)

Space (2002)

Adaline Falling Star (2000)

Tigers at Twilight (1999)

Standing in the Light: The Captive Diary of Catherine Carey Logan, Delaware Valley, Pennsylvania, 1763 (1998)

Dolphins at Daybreak (1997)

One World, Many Religions: The Ways We Worship (1996)

Mermaid Tales from around the World (1993)

Spider Kane and the Mystery at Jumbo Nightcrawler's (1993)

Dinosaurs before Dark (1992)

American Tall Tales (1990)

Favorite Greek Myths (1989)

Run, Run As Fast As You Can (1982)

Osborne's Major Literary Award

1997 Orbis Pictus Honor Book
One World, Many Religions: The Ways We Worship

"*Twenty years and forty books later, I feel I'm one of the most fortunate people on earth. I've journeyed through Greek mythology, Norse mythology, medieval stories, and American tall tales. I've 'met' George Washington and Ben Franklin, and without leaving home, I've traveled around the globe, learning about world religions.*"

the hospital, and had to return to the United States.

Back home, she went to work as a travel consultant in Washington, D.C. One night she went to see a play. As she watched the play, she fell in love with one of the actors, Will Osborne. They met, and she married him about one year later.

After her marriage, Mary Pope Osborne traveled with her husband. He was in plays and productions across the United States. One day she decided to try writing a book. When she completed the story, she showed it to an editor who was very pleased with it. Osborne's first book for young people, *Run, Run As Fast As You Can,* was published in 1982. She has gone on to write many other books for children and young people.

Osborne has written more than twenty-five books in the Magic Tree House series. The stories are about two kids who discover a tree house full

WHEN OSBORNE BECAME ILL DURING HER TRIP THROUGH ASIA, SHE READ ALL THREE BOOKS OF J. R. R. TOLKIEN'S LORD OF THE RINGS TRILOGY.

of books. Each one of the books lets them magically go to different times and places. In her books, Osborne helps her readers learn about history, people, and places throughout the world.

Osborne continues to write books for children and young people. She lives with her husband in Connecticut and in their cabin in Pennsylvania.

> *"The wonderful thing about a career as a children's book writer is that there are so many different forms in which to fill different sorts of content. Choosing the vehicle that will carry a new story or passion into the world is half the fun."*

❧

WHERE TO FIND OUT MORE ABOUT MARY POPE OSBORNE

BOOKS

Cullinan, Bernice E., and Diane G. Person, eds. *Continuum Encyclopedia of Children's Literature*. New York: Continuum, 2001.

Rockman, Connie C., ed. *Eighth Book of Junior Authors and Illustrators*. New York: H. W. Wilson Company, 2000.

WEB SITES

KIDSREAD.COM
http://www.kidsreads.com/authors/au-osborne-mary-pope.asp
To read an interview with Osborne and other information about her life

MARY POPE OBSORNE HOME PAGE
http://www.marypopeosborne.com/
To read biographical information and a list of works

———

OSBORNE RECEIVES MORE THAN **500** LETTERS EACH MONTH FROM MEMBERS OF THE MAGIC TREE HOUSE FAN CLUB.

Helen Oxenbury

Born: June 2, 1938

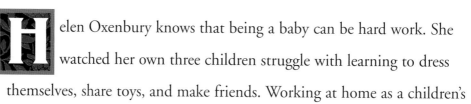

Helen Oxenbury knows that being a baby can be hard work. She watched her own three children struggle with learning to dress themselves, share toys, and make friends. Working at home as a children's book illustrator, Oxenbury began to wonder why there were no books made just for babies. Finally, Helen Oxenbury sat down at her drawing table and created her own version of a perfect baby book. Almost as soon as Oxenbury's first titles were published, they began flying out of bookstores and into the hands (and mouths) of grateful babies.

Helen Oxenbury was born on June 2, 1938, in Suffolk, England, just before the start of the World War II (1939–1945). Suffolk, she says,

---

OXENBURY GREW UP IN ENGLAND DURING WORLD WAR II
AND REMEMBERS DRINKING TEA WITH HER FAMILY IN THE GARDEN AT
NIGHT AFTER AIR-RAID SIRENS REQUIRED THEM TO EVACUATE THE HOUSE.

inspired her to become an artist. Sometimes the sky was clear, and other times it was gray and gloomy, but it always made an impression on her.

Her parents encouraged Helen's early love of drawing. Her father, an architect, picked out her best pictures, and entered them in drawing contests. Helen usually won—exactly as her father expected. When she told her parents that, instead of going to college, she planned to attend art school in London, they happily agreed with her plan.

In London, she became close friends with John Burningham, a fellow art student studying illustration. Oxenbury longed for a career in theater design. When she finished school, she took a job with a small theater company. She loved creating bold, bright designs that gave audiences a sense of being in a different world.

> *"I can't remember any bedtime stories my father made up. I think these were potentially very good, but he had the maddening habit of dropping off to sleep before the end."*

Oxenbury and Burningham married in 1964. They had their first child a few years later. As a new mother, Oxenbury found her long hours at the theater difficult. Burningham, who was a well-known children's book illustrator, encouraged Oxenbury to try creating her own books.

So Oxenbury started working as a children's book illustrator. In time, she began work on her first book especially for babies. Babies, she

---

OXENBURY GREW UP A GREAT FAN OF THE BABAR
BOOKS BY JEAN AND LAURENT DE BRUNHOFF.

A Selected Bibliography of Oxenbury's Work

Helen Oxenbury Nursery Collection (2004)

Helen Oxbenbury's Big Baby Book (2003)

Big Momma Makes the World (2002)

Alice's Adventures in Wonderland (Illustrations only, 1999)

It's My Birthday (1994)

The Three Little Wolves and the Big Bad Pig (Illustrations only, 1993)

We're Going on a Bear Hunt (Illustrations only, 1989)

Pippo Gets Lost (1988)

Clap Hands (1987)

Say Goodnight (1987)

Tickle, Tickle (1987)

I Hear (1986)

Playing (1981)

The Dragon of an Ordinary Family (Illustrations only, 1969)

The Quangle Wangle's Hat (Illustrations only, 1969)

Numbers of Things (1968)

Oxenbury's Major Literary Awards

2003 Boston Globe-Horn Book Picture Book
  Big Momma Makes the World

1999 Kate Greenaway Medal
  Alice's Adventures in Wonderland

1969 Kate Greenaway Medal
  The Dragon of an Ordinary Family
  The Quangle Wangle's Hat

knew, need books small enough to fit in their tiny hands yet sturdy enough to withstand chewing. Babies also like simple drawings in clear, bright colors. She showed her book to friends in the publishing business. They agreed that board books for babies were a great idea whose time had come.

In 1969, Oxenbury won her first Kate Greenaway Medal for her illustrations of *The Quangle Wangle's Hat* by Edward Lear and *The Dragon of an Ordinary Family* by Margaret Mahy. Oxenbury's other well-known titles include *We're Going on a Bear Hunt, Say Goodnight, Clap Hands,* and many books featuring the characters Tom and Pippo. Tom is a young boy, and

Pippo, a stuffed monkey, is Tom's constant companion and very loyal friend.

In the late 1990s, Oxenbury created illustrations for a new version of Lewis Carroll's *Alice's Adventures in Wonderland.* Using a combination of watercolor and black-and-white line drawings, she made Alice a confident, fearless modern girl. She was truly surprised when, in 1999, she was again awarded the Kate Greenaway Medal.

> *"When I actually began to illustrate, with* Numbers of Things, *I found it enormously satisfying, and seven books . . . four years, and two children later, I still find it so."*

WHERE TO FIND OUT MORE ABOUT HELEN OXENBURY

BOOKS

De Montreville, Davis, and Donna Hill, eds. *Third Book of Junior Authors.* New York: H.W. Wilson Company, 1972.

McElmeel, Sharron L. *100 Most Popular Picture Book Authors and Illustrators: Biographical Sketches and Bibliographies.* Englewood, Colo.: Libraries Unlimited, 2000.

WEB SITE
HALL KIDS ILLUSTRATORS
http://hallkidsillustrators.com/O/9.shtml
To find a list of Helen Oxenbury's titles with links to summaries and reviews

---

OXENBURY HATED SCHOOL, BUT SHE ENJOYED TENNIS AND PLAYED IT ALMOST CONSTANTLY BEFORE TAKING ART CLASSES AT IPSWICH SCHOOL OF ART.

Barbara Park

Born: April 27, 1947

Have you ever known anyone so skinny that you called him Skinnybones? Have you ever known someone who couldn't play baseball but just kept trying? Do you think it is funny to call your school bus the stupid smelly bus? Well, Barbara Park thinks all these things are very funny indeed. Her stories are full of children who suffer taunts and who don't quite fit in. They are normal kids, and their world, though sometimes painful, is full of comedy.

Barbara Park was born on April 27, 1947, in Mount Holly, New Jersey. Her father was a banker and a business entrepreneur. Her mother worked as a school secretary. As a child, Barbara wanted to be

PARK SAYS SHE RARELY TAKES MORE THAN TWO MONTHS TO WRITE A JUNIE B. JONES BOOK. *MICK HARTE WAS HERE*, HOWEVER, TOOK ALMOST TWO YEARS TO WRITE!

a singer or an actress. She did not like reading very much. In school, Barbara made the class laugh and got in trouble for interrupting.

It was humor that led her into writing. She realized that the written word could be as entertaining as the spoken word. She attended Rider College (now University) in Lawrenceville, New Jersey, and then the University of Alabama, where she read a lot and practiced her skills as a writer.

In 1969, the year she graduated, she married Richard A. Park. The couple later had two sons, Steven Allen and David Matthew. Those two sons gave Barbara Park a direct connection to the childhood world she found so funny. She could also try out her humor on her sons.

> *"I always found myself incredibly amusing. So from the first grade on, whenever a funny thought hit me, I would happily blurt it out for the whole class to hear."*

While her sons were growing up, Park decided to write down her funny stories. In 1981, the first one, *Don't Make Me Smile,* was published. Her tone was refreshing from the start. Park's characters talked like kids and got into hilarious situations. They acted badly—sometimes spoiled—but their good sides showed through, too.

IN PARK'S SERIES THE GEEK CHRONICLES, THREE KIDS COMPETE FOR THE HONOR OF BEING LEAST POPULAR IN THEIR CLASS: MAXIE GETS PERFECT GRADES; ROSIE LIKES TO GOSSIP; AND EARL LACKS COURAGE.

A Selected Bibliography of Park's Work

Junie B., First Grader: Aloha-ha-ha! (2006)

Junie B., First Grader: Jingle Bells, Batman Smells! (P.S. So Does Mary) (2005)

Junie B., First Grader: Shipwrecked (2004)

Junie B., First Grader: Toothless Wonder (2002)

Junie B., First Grader at Last! (2001)

The Graduation of Jake Moon (2000)

Junie B. Jones Smells Something Fishy (1998)

Psssst! It's Me—the Bogeyman (1998)

Junie B. Jones Loves Handsome Warren (1996)

Mick Harte Was Here (1995)

Junie B. Jones and the Stupid Smelly Bus (1992)

Rosie Swanson: Fourth-Grade Geek for President (1991)

My Mother Got Married: And Other Disasters (1989)

Almost Starring Skinnybones (1988)

The Kid in the Red Jacket (1987)

Buddies (1985)

Beanpole (1983)

Operation, Dump the Chump (1982)

Skinnybones (1982)

Don't Make Me Smile (1981)

Park has always avoided including heavy messages about childhood. Instead, she lets the humor of her books speak for itself.

One of Park's most popular characters is the kindergarten-and-then-first-grade misfit Junie B. Jones. Much goes wrong in the world of Junie B., whose adventures are chronicled in a series of short chapter books.

Not all of Park's books are humorous. In *The Graduation of Jake Moon,* a boy struggles

> *"I don't believe that in order to be worthwhile a book must try to teach some weighty lesson in life."*

to cope with his grandfather's Alzheimer's disease. In *Mick Harte Was Here,* Park writes about the death of a sibling.

Whatever the topic, Park writes stories full of humor and truth. There are many more stories to come from this best-selling author.

❧

Where to Find Out More about Barbara Park

Books

McElmeel, Sharron L. *100 Most Popular Children's Authors: Biographical Sketches and Bibliographies.* Englewood, Colo.: Libraries Unlimited, 1999.

Silvey, Anita, ed. *The Essential Guide to Children's Books and Their Creators.* Boston: Houghton Mifflin Company, 2002.

Something about the Author, Vol. 78.
Detroit: Gale Research, 1999.

Web Sites

Educational Paperback Association
http://edupaperback.org/showauth.cfm?authid=38
To read about Barbara Park's life and works

Meet Junie B. Jones
http://www.randomhouse.com/kids/junieb/
The personal Web site of Park's fictional character Junie B. Jones

Random House Kids
http://www.randomhouse.com/kids/junieb/author/author.html
To read a biography of Barbara Park

Park says that J. D. Salinger's *The Catcher in the Rye* was the first book she read that felt like a person, not a book. She has always tried to capture the same life in her books.

Linda Sue Park

Born: March 25, 1960

"If you want to be a writer," says Linda Sue Park, "you have to read A LOT. Reading is training for writers the same way that working out is training for athletes!"

Linda Sue Park was born in Urbana, Illinois, in 1960. Her father, a computer analyst, and her mother, a teacher, were both immigrants from Korea. The family lived in Park Forest, a suburb of Chicago, Illinois.

Linda Sue began writing poems and stories when she was only four. Her first poem was published when she was nine. It was a haiku—a type of Japanese poem with seventeen syllables. She was paid one dollar for that poem. Her father framed the check, and it still hangs above his desk.

———

PARK'S DOG IS A BORDER TERRIER NAMED FERGUS.

Linda Sue published more poems throughout her elementary and high school years. She attended Stanford University in California, where she majored in English.

After graduation, Park landed a job writing for an oil company. Oil was not her favorite subject, but she says the job taught her to make any subject interesting.

Park moved to Dublin, Ireland, in her twenties. There she studied at Trinity College. She also fell in love with an Irishman named Ben Dobbin, whom she married in 1984. The couple then moved to London, England, where they had two children. During that

A Selected Bibliography of Park's Work

The Archer's Quest (2006)
Bee-Bim Bop! (2005)
Project Mulberry (2005)
What Does Bunny See? A Book of Colors and Flowers (2005)
Yum! Yuck! A Foldout Book of People Sounds (2005)
Mung-Mung: A Foldout Book of Animal Sounds (2004)
Firekeeper's Son (2003)
When My Name Was Keoko (2002)
A Single Shard (2001)
The Kite Fighters (2000)
Seesaw Girl (1999)

Park's Major Literary Awards

2002 Newbery Medal
  A Single Shard

time, Park also worked as a food journalist and taught English as a second language. After seven years in London, the family moved back to the United States.

Finally, Park realized that writing children's books was what she wanted to do. She was excited to see her first novel, *Seesaw Girl*, published in 1999. Like many of Park's stories, it is set in Korea. Its heroine, Jade Blossom, is a twelve-year-old girl living in the 1600s. She longs to know what lies beyond the walls of her home. Park's next novel was *The Kite Fighters*. This book was special for her because her father did the illustrations for the chapter openings.

> *"I have been writing all my life, but only after I had children of my own did I feel the desire to explore my ethnic heritage (Korean) through writing."*

Park's third novel, *A Single Shard*, really brought her into the limelight. It won the Newbery Medal for children's literature in 2002. *A Single Shard* tells the story of an orphan boy in twelfth-century Korea. More than anything, he wants to learn how to make celadon, a special type of pottery with a greenish glaze, from an old master. Park weaves her fictional story around factual material. "Every [pottery] piece described in the book actually exists in a museum or private collection somewhere in the world," she says.

PARK ENJOYS COOKING, TRAVELING, WATCHING SPORTS, PLAYING TRIVIA GAMES, AND WORKING ON *NEW YORK TIMES* CROSSWORD PUZZLES.

More novels and several picture books followed *A Single Shard*. Park has many other children's books in the works.

Park lives in Upstate New York with her husband, their two children, a dog, a hamster, and several tadpoles.

✎

WHERE TO FIND OUT MORE ABOUT LINDA SUE PARK

BOOKS

McElmeel, Sharron L. *Children's Authors and Illustrators Too Good to Miss: Biographical Sketches and Bibliographies*. Englewood, Colo: Libraries Unlimited, 2004.

Rockman, Connie C., ed. *The Ninth Book of Junior Authors and Illustrators*. New York: H. W. Wilson Company, 2004.

Silvey, Anita, ed. *The Essential Guide to Children's Books and Their Creators*. Boston: Houghton Mifflin Company, 2002.

Sutherland, Zena. *Children and Books*. 9th ed. Boston: Allyn & Bacon, 1997.

WEB SITES

CHILDREN'S AND YOUNG ADULT LITERATURE RESOURCES
http://www.cynthialeitichsmith.com/lit_resources/authors/interviews/LindaSuePark.html
To read an interview of the award-winning author

KIDS READS.COM
http://www.kidsreads.com/authors/au-park-linda-sue.asp
To read a biography of Linda Sue Park

LINDA SUE PARK
http://www.lspark.com/
For a biography, book information, activities, and links to other sites

PARK FIRST VISITED KOREA AT AGE TWELVE. THERE SHE MET ONE OF HER AUNTS, WHO LIVED IN A TRADITIONAL KOREAN HOUSE BUILT AROUND A SMALL COURTYARD. PARK USED A VERSION OF THAT HOUSE IN *SEESAW GIRL*.

Robert Andrew Parker

Born: May 14, 1927

As a famous artist, Robert Andrew Parker has exhibited his artwork all over the world. Even some kings and queens have his paintings in their private collections! Among his many subjects are landscapes, seascapes, people, and animals. While pursuing his career as an artist, Parker has also managed to illustrate more than fifty books for children.

Robert Andrew Parker was born on May 14, 1927, in Norfolk, Virginia. Not much is known about his early life. In 1948, Parker enrolled in art classes at the School of the Art Institute of Chicago. That same year, he and Dorothy Lane Daniels were married. Over the years, they had five sons—Christopher, Anthony, Eric, Geoffrey, and Nicholas.

After earning his degree in art education in 1952, Parker studied briefly at the Skowhegan School of Painting and Sculpture in Skowhegan, Maine. Then he moved to New York City, where he studied at the Atelier

ONE OF PARKER'S HOBBIES IS PLAYING THE DRUMS WITH JAZZ MUSICIANS.

76

17 studio from 1952 to 1953. Around that same time, the city's art galleries began exhibiting his paintings.

In 1955, Parker was teaching high-school art in Westchester County, New York, when he got a strange phone call. He was asked to have his hands photographed. The Metro-Goldwyn-Mayer film studio was preparing to make the film *Lust for Life*. It was the life story of

> *"I learned a lot copying van Gogh's work and of course I greatly admired him. He took more risks with color than anyone before him."*

the famous artist Vincent van Gogh, with Kirk Douglas in the starring role. Someone had recommended that Parker be hired to create paintings in van Gogh's style that would appear in the movie. But it was important for Parker's hands to look similar to Kirk Douglas's hands. Then Parker's hands could be filmed in the act of painting. With skillful film editing, it would look as if Kirk Douglas were painting the art himself.

Parker's hands passed the test. He got the job and took off for France for filming. As it turned out, his hands were never shown in the completed film. But he learned a lot from copying so many van Gogh paintings. Parker later made paintings for other films, as well as

---

PARKER LOVES TO TRAVEL, AND SOME OF HIS PAINTINGS REFLECT PLACES HE HAS SEEN IN NEW MEXICO, PANAMA, IRELAND, AND ASIA'S HIMALAYA MOUNTAINS.

A Selected Bibliography of Parker's Work

Ballet of the Elephants (Illustrations only, 2006)

Marooned: The Strange but True Adventures of Alexander Selkirk, the Real Robinson Crusoe (Illustrations only, 2005)

Orville: A Dog Story (Illustrations only, 2003)

Action Jackson (Illustrations only, 2002)

To Fly: The Story of the Wright Brothers (Illustrations only, 2002)

Who Was Albert Einstein? (Illustrations only, 2002)

The Charterhouse of Parma (Illustrations only, 2000)

Cold Feet (Illustrations only, 2000)

The Hatmaker's Sign: A Story by Benjamin Franklin (Illustrations only, 2000)

Sleds on Boston Common: A Story from the American Revolution (Illustrations only, 2000)

Stowaway (Illustrations only, 2000)

Just Juice (Illustrations only, 1998)

Aunt Skilly and the Stranger (Illustrations only, 1994)

Grandfather Tang's Story (Illustrations only, 1990)

The Dancing Skeleton (Illustrations only, 1989)

The Whistling Skeleton (Illustrations only, 1982)

Liam's Catch (Illustrations only, 1972)

Pop Corn and Ma Goodness (Illustrations only, 1969)

Ponies for Hire (Illustrations only, 1967)

Parker's Major Literary Awards

2003 Boston Globe-Horn Book Nonfiction Honor Book
2003 Orbus Pictus Honor Book
   To Fly: The Story of the Wright Brothers

2001 Boston Globe-Horn Book Picture Book Award
   Cold Feet

1970 Caldecott Honor Book
   Pop Corn and Ma Goodness

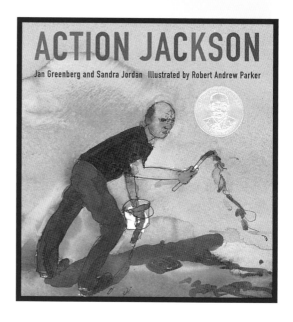

creating numerous movie sets, backdrops, and costume designs.

Parker spent much of his career teaching art. From 1960 to 1970, he taught at the School of Visual Arts in New York City. During this time, he began illustrating books. His first illustrated children's book, published in 1967, was *Ponies for Hire* by Margaret

MacPherson. He went on to illustrate dozens of books over the next forty years.

Parker especially enjoyed illustrating *Action Jackson* by Jan Greenberg and Sandra Jordan. It's a biography of the modern artist Jackson Pollock, whose nickname was Action Jackson. Parker himself had known Pollock as a young man. Parker used vibrant watercolors to portray Pollock swirling and splattering paint on a canvas.

Parker continues to illustrate children's books as he pursues his fine art. He lives in West Cornwall, Connecticut.

❧

WHERE TO FIND OUT MORE ABOUT ROBERT ANDREW PARKER

BOOK
Silvey, Anita, ed. *The Essential Guide to Children's Books and Their Creators*. Boston: Houghton Mifflin Company, 2002.

WEB SITE
HOUGHTON MIFFLIN
http://www.houghtonmifflinbooks.com/booksellers/press_release/kimmel/
For a press release for *Orville: A Dog Story* and a biography of the artist

TWO OF THE MONARCHS WHO OWN PAINTINGS BY PARKER ARE KING GUSTAV OF SWEDEN AND QUEEN ELIZABETH II OF THE UNITED KINGDOM.

Dorothy Hinshaw Patent

Born: April 30, 1940

"I knew that I loved animals, the woods, and exploring, and I always wanted to learn everything possible about something that interested me. But I never yearned to be a writer," says Dorothy Hinshaw Patent. As a girl, she read only nonfiction and stories about horses and dogs. She kept snakes, lizards, and fish for pets. Each spring she collected tadpoles and kept them while they turned into toads.

Dorothy Hinshaw was born on April 30, 1940, in Rochester, Minnesota. She lived there until she was nine years old, while her father worked as a doctor at the famous Mayo Clinic. Then the family moved to California. She studied biology at Stanford University, then earned a Ph.D. degree in zoology in 1968 from the University of California–Berkeley. She met her future husband, Greg Patent, at Berkeley.

PATENT HAS TWO DOGS: ELSA (NAMED FOR THE
LION IN THE FAMOUS BOOK AND MOVIE *BORN FREE*) AND NINJA.

Patent worked for a while as a scientist, but after she had two sons, Jason and David, she wanted to find a way to work at home. She tried writing children's science books, and after a couple of unsuccessful attempts, she got a contract to write a book—about weasels. By this time Patent and her family lived in Missoula, Montana, where her husband was a professor at the University of Montana.

Weasels, Otters, Skunks, and Their Family was published in 1973. It was the first of more than 100 books by Patent. Most of her books are about animals: worms, spiders, prairie dogs, whales, buffalo, wild turkeys, and many more.

LOOKING AT BEARS

DOROTHY HINSHAW PATENT
photographs by
WILLIAM MUÑOZ

A Selected Bibliography of Patent's Work

Buffalo and Indians: A Shared Destiny (2006)
Brown Pelicans (2005)
Right Dog for the Job: Ira's Path From Service to Guide Dog (2004)
Colorful Captivating Coral Reefs (2003)
Animals on the Trial with Lewis and Clark (2002)
The Lewis and Clark Trail: Then and Now (2002)
Rainforest Animals (2002)
The Bald Eagle Returns (2000)
Fire: Friend or Foe (1998)
Alex and Friends: Animal Talk, Animal Thinking (1998)
Flashy Fantastic Rain Forest Frogs (1997)
Biodiversity (1996)
Looking at Bears (1994)
The Vanishing Feast: How Dwindling Genetic Diversity Threatens the World's Food Supply (1994)
Killer Whales (1993)
Feathers (1992)
The Challenge of Extinction (1991)
Appaloosa Horses (1988)
All about Whales (1987)
Germs! (1983)
Spider Magic (1982)
The World of Worms (1978)
Evolution Goes On Every Day (1977)
How Insects Communicate (1975)
Weasels, Otters, Skunks, and Their Family (1973)

> "*I believe . . .we owe our existence to the earth, and it is the balance of nature that sustains all life; we upset that balance at our peril. I believe well-informed children can grow into responsible citizens capable of making the wise but difficult decisions necessary for the survival of a livable world.*"

Sometimes the process of researching and writing one book leads to another. For instance, for a book about animal intelligence, Patent met a woman who was training a parrot to understand the meaning of words. That led to *Alex and Friends: Animal Talk, Animal Thinking. The Vanishing Feast: How Dwindling Genetic Diversity Threatens the World's Food Supply,* a book about the food chain and genetics, led to *Biodiversity,* a broader look at the same subject.

Since the 1980s, Patent has often worked with the photographer William Muñoz, who also used to live in Missoula. Recently, in honor of the 100th anniversary of the Lewis and Clark expedition, the two traveled the route the explorers took across western North America in the early 1800s. The result was three books about the expedition's history, plants, and animals.

Most of Patent's books are sold to schools and libraries rather than in bookstores. Patent believes that publishers don't think they can make money from science books, so they don't want to publish them. She has written that children's science books are "an endangered species."

———

PATENT'S BEST-SELLING BOOK IS *FLASHY FANTASTIC RAIN FOREST FROGS,* A PICTURE BOOK ILLUSTRATED BY KENDAHL JAN JUBB. IT HAS SOLD 300,000 COPIES.

Patent and her husband live in a house near Blue Mountain in Montana. Its windows look out on the mountains and the Missoula Valley. Across the street is a meadow that is national forestland. "It's a perfect place for a person who loves nature to live," she says.

"When I was young, there was a feeling science had done it all, and there was nothing left to discover . . . when I got in college, it was clear there was. DNA was discovered. It was an exciting time for biologists. I want kids to feel there are new challenges."

WHERE TO FIND OUT MORE ABOUT DOROTHY HINSHAW PATENT

BOOKS

Holtze, Sally Holmes, ed. *Sixth Book of Junior Authors & Illustrators.* New York: H. W. Wilson Company, 1989.

Something about the Author. Autobiography Series, Vol. 13. Detroit: Gale Research, 1991.

WEB SITES

AMERICAN COLLECTION
http://www.ncteamericancollection.org/litmap/patent_dorothy_mt.htm
To read an article about Dorothy Hinshaw Patent's life

DOROTHY HINSHAW PATENT HOME PAGE
http://www.dorothyhinshawpatent.com/
To read a biography of Dorothy Hinshaw Patent and information on her books

NOT MANY WRITERS GET TO COMPLETE 100 BOOKS, AS PATENT HAS. HER 100TH WAS *FIRE: FRIEND OR FOE,* WHICH EXPLAINED THE ROLE OF FIRES IN PRESERVING FORESTS.

Katherine Paterson

Born: October 31, 1932

When she was a young girl, Katherine Paterson did not think about becoming a writer. She was much more interested in being a movie star or a missionary. Paterson changed her mind when she became an adult, and she's now an award-winning children's author. Her best-known books include *The Great Gilly Hopkins, Bridge to Terabithia, The Master Puppeteer,* and *Jacob Have I Loved.*

She was born Katherine Womeldorf in 1932 in Qing Jiang, China. Her parents were Christian missionaries. Her family lived in China until the start of World War II (1939–1945), when they moved back to the United States.

As a little girl, Katherine loved to read. Her mother would read books

THREE OF PATERSON'S BOOKS—*THE GREAT GILLY HOPKINS, BRIDGE TO TERABITHIA,* AND *JACOB HAVE I LOVED*—HAVE BEEN ADAPTED FOR TELEVISION.

to her every day. Katherine learned to read before she began school. She learned to write shortly after she started school, and she loved writing stories and poems. She had a story published in the school newspaper in China when she was seven years old.

> *"Reading was where I could always find friends. I learned to trust books, and to love books, and to find a great deal of comfort from books when I was quite young."*

Katherine Womeldorf attended Kings College in Tennessee, where she majored in English literature. Many of her teachers recognized her writing talent. They encouraged her to pursue a career as a writer. After college, she went to work as a sixth-grade teacher at a school in rural Virginia. A few years later, she returned to college to study Bible and Christian education. In 1957, she went to Japan to work for the pastors of several churches.

The young woman loved Japan and planned to live there the rest of her life. Then, in 1961, she received a scholarship to study at a school in New York City. She met John Barstow Paterson and married him in the summer of 1962. She did not return to Japan but has wonderful memories of her time there.

Katherine Paterson became a full-time writer in 1964. In the early years of her career, she was also busy raising her four children. Her first

---

PATERSON IS THE MOTHER OF TWO SONS AND TWO ADOPTED DAUGHTERS. ONE OF HER DAUGHTERS WAS BORN IN HONG KONG, AND THE OTHER WAS BORN ON AN APACHE INDIAN RESERVATION IN ARIZONA.

A Selected Bibliography of Paterson's Work

Bread and Roses, Too (2006)

The Same Stuff As Stars (2002)

The Field of the Dogs (2001)

The Wide-Awake Princess (2000)

Celia and the Sweet, Sweet Water (1998)

The Angel and the Donkey (1996)

Jip: His Story (1996)

Lyddie (1991)

The Tale of the Mandarin Ducks (1990)

Park's Quest (1988)

Consider the Lilies: Plants of the Bible (1986)

Jacob Have I Loved (1980)

Angels & Other Strangers: Family Christmas Stories (1979)

The Great Gilly Hopkins (1978)

Bridge to Terabithia (1977)

The Master Puppeteer (1975)

Of Nightingales That Weep (1974)

The Sign of the Chrysanthemum (1973)

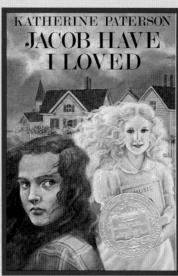

Paterson's Major Literary Awards

1998 Hans Christian Andersen Medal for Authors

1997 Scott O'Dell Award
Jip: His Story

1991 Boston Globe–Horn Book Picture Book Award
The Tale of the Mandarin Ducks

1981 Newbery Medal
Jacob Have I Loved

1979 National Book Award
1979 Newbery Honor Book
The Great Gilly Hopkins

1978 Newbery Medal
Bridge to Terabithia

1977 National Book Award
The Master Puppeteer

published writing was curriculum materials for church schools. Her first book for children, *The Sign of the Chrysanthemum,* was published in 1973. Her first three books were historical fiction set in Japan.

Even though she did not want to be a writer as a child, Paterson loves being a writer now. "My aim is to engage young readers in the life of a story which came out of me but which is not mine, but ours," Paterson says. "I know that without the efforts of my

"My gift seems to be that I am one of those fortunate people who can, if she works hard at it, uncover a story that children will enjoy."

reader, I have accomplished nothing. I have not written a book for children unless the book is brought to life by the child who reads it."

Paterson has written more than twenty-five books for children and young people. Her books have been translated into more than fifteen languages. She currently lives in Vermont and is still writing books for young people.

❧

WHERE TO FIND OUT MORE ABOUT KATHERINE PATERSON

BOOKS

Cary, Alice. *Katherine Paterson.* Santa Barbara, Calif.: Learning Works, 1997.

Kovacs, Deborah, and James Preller. *Meet the Authors and Illustrators: 60 Creators of Favorite Children's Books Talk about Their Work.* Vol. 1. New York: Scholastic, 1991.

McElmeel, Sharron L. *100 Most Popular Children's Authors: Biographical Sketches and Bibliographies.* Englewood, Colo.: Libraries Unlimited, 1999.

Schmidt, Gary D. *Katherine Paterson.* New York: Twayne, 1994.

WEB SITES

EDUCATIONAL PAPERBACK ASSOCIATION
http://edupaperback.org/showauth.cfm?authid=60
To read autobiographical and other information about Katherine Paterson

INTERNET PUBLIC LIBRARY
http://ipl.si.umich.edu/kidspace/askauthor/paterson.html
To read biographical information about Katherine Paterson

KATHERINE PATERSON HOME PAGE
http://www.terabithia.com/
To read extensive information about Katherine Paterson

———

ALONG WITH WRITING HER OWN BOOKS FOR CHILDREN AND YOUNG PEOPLE, PATERSON HAS TRANSLATED TWO BOOKS WRITTEN BY JAPANESE AUTHORS INTO ENGLISH.

Gary Paulsen

Born: May 17, 1939

ary Paulsen is the author of more than 175 books for adults and children. He has also written more than 200 short stories and articles for magazines. His books are very popular among young people. Paulsen's best-known books for children and young people include *Hatchet, Dancing Carl, The Winter Room, Dogsong,* and *The Crossing.*

Gary Paulsen was born on May 17, 1939, in Minneapolis, Minnesota. Life as a child was not easy for Gary. His parents were alcoholics, and he was often left alone. He was very shy and did not have many friends at school. Gary's father was in the military, so the Paulsen family moved many times. Gary often lived with his grandmother or his aunts.

BEFORE BECOMING A FULL-TIME WRITER, PAULSEN WORKED AS A TEACHER, AN ACTOR, A DIRECTOR, A FARMER, A RANCHER, A TRUCK DRIVER, A TRAPPER, A PROFESSIONAL ARCHER, A MIGRANT FARMWORKER, AND A SAILOR.

When Gary was a young boy, reading became a passion for him. One night he was walking in the small northern Minnesota town where he lived. The temperature was very cold. Gary was looking for a place to get warm. He entered the public library. The librarian asked Gary if he wanted a library card. He checked out his first book, and he became hooked on reading. "The librarian kept giving me books," Paulsen says. "At first

"It's like things have come full circle. I felt like nothing the first time I walked into a library, and now library associations are giving me awards. It means a lot to me."

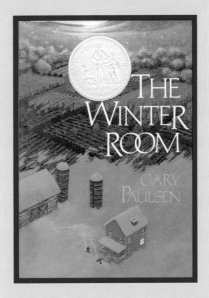

A Selected Bibliography of Paulsen's Work

Time Hackers (2005)
Brian's Hunt (2003)
Woodsong (2002)
Escape (2000)
Brian's Return (1999)
My Life in Dog Years (1998)
Brian's Winter (1996)
The Tortilla Factory (1995)
Nightjohn (1993)
The River (1991)
The Winter Room (1989)
The Island (1988)
Hatchet (1987)
The Crossing (1987)
Dogsong (1985)
Dancing Carl (1983)
The Spitball Gang (1980)
The Green Recruit (1978)
Tiltawhirl John (1977)
Winterkill (1976)

Paulsen's Major Literary Awards

1990 Newbery Honor Book
  The Winter Room

1988 Newbery Honor Book
  Hatchet

1986 Newbery Honor Book
  Dogsong

"*I read myself to sleep every night. And I don't think of any of the good things that have happened to me would have been possible without that librarian and libraries in general.*"

it took me a month to read a book, then two weeks, then a week, and pretty soon I was reading two books a week." Gary spent many hours in the basement of his apartment building reading books.

Gary ran away from home when he was fourteen years old. He joined a traveling carnival. This experience gave him a sense of adventure. After attending college for a short time, Paulsen joined the army in 1958. He served in the army until 1962.

Then he worked at many different jobs while he pursued his career as a writer. He finally left his job as a satellite technician and went to work as a magazine proofreader. Paulsen worked on his own writing at night. After doing this for a year, he returned to Minnesota. He rented a cabin by a lake and worked on his first novel for adults.

Paulsen became a full-time writer in the 1960s. He has written plays, magazine articles, and fiction and nonfiction books for both adults and young people.

Paulsen's love for the outdoors and nature are powerful themes in his books. Many of his books for young people are set in the

PAULSEN TWICE PARTICIPATED IN THE IDITAROD, A 1,200-MILE DOGSLED RACE THAT GOES FROM ANCHORAGE, ALASKA, TO NOME, ALASKA.

wilderness. His characters often overcome difficult challenges. Paulsen also uses his own experiences dogsledding, hunting, and trapping in his books.

Today, Paulsen lives in New Mexico with his wife. He continues to write fiction and nonfiction books for adults and young people.

ॐ

WHERE TO FIND OUT MORE ABOUT GARY PAULSEN

BOOKS

Kovacs, Deborah, and James Preller. *Meet the Authors and Illustrators: 60 Creators of Favorite Children's Books Talk about Their Work.* Vol. 1. New York: Scholastic, 1991.

McElmeel, Sharron L. *100 Most Popular Children's Authors: Biographical Sketches and Bibliographies.* Englewood, Colo.: Libraries Unlimited, 1999.

Paulsen, Gary. *My Life in Dog Years.* New York: Delacorte Press, 1998.

Silvey, Anita, ed. *The Essential Guide to Children's Books and Their Creators.* Boston: Houghton Mifflin Company, 2002.

WEB SITES

EDUCATIONAL PAPERBACK ASSOCIATION
http://edupaperback.org/showauth.cfm?authid=67
To read a biography of Gary Paulsen

RANDOM HOUSE
http://www.randomhouse.com/features/garypaulsen/
To read an interview with Gary Paulsen

PAULSEN SPENDS A GREAT DEAL OF TIME ON HIS WRITING. HE OFTEN WORKS EIGHTEEN TO TWENTY HOURS EACH DAY WHEN HE IS WORKING ON A BOOK.

Richard Peck

Born: April 5, 1934

Richard Peck knows about young people. For many years, Peck was a teacher. He listened to what his students had to say. He heard them talk about their hopes, their dreams, and their heartaches. Now Peck writes for young adults everywhere. Since 1971, he has written more than twenty novels for young adults—mysteries, comedies, and stories of the supernatural. Many of Peck's books focus on the problems that young  people face today, including peer pressure, sexual assault, and suicide. In all of his novels, Peck tries to send kids a strong message: to grow up, you must break away from your peers and think for yourself.

Richard Peck was born on April 5, 1934, in Decatur, Illinois. Peck says that he grew up listening. At the dinner table, he listened as his

---

IN 1995, PECK WROTE HIS AUTOBIOGRAPHY. IT IS CALLED *ANONYMOUSLY YOURS.*

father, his mother, and his aunt talked about current events. At bedtime, he listened while his mother read him stories. Richard also listened to the radio. There was no television in the house when he was growing up, so Richard created images of what he heard in his head. Listening carefully to others would later help Richard with his writing.

"I want to write novels that ask honest questions about serious issues. A novel is never an answer; it's always a question."

In 1956, Peck graduated from college in Indiana. He entered the army and spent two years in Germany. It was there that Peck began his writing career. As an assistant to the army chaplain, Peck often wrote the chaplain's sermons. After he left the army, Peck returned to Illinois, where he taught high school for a time. Then, in 1965, Peck decided to make one of his dreams come true: he moved to New York.

In 1971, Peck quit his teaching job and began writing his first novel. The book, *Don't Look and It Won't Hurt,* was for young adults. It was about teen pregnancy. In 1992, the book was made into a movie called *Gas Food Lodging*.

Peck likes to write books that make kids think. In many of his stories, the main characters are young adults. Peck puts his characters into situations in which they must fend for themselves. He hopes that

PECK RESEARCHES HIS CHARACTERS AND SETTINGS BY LOOKING THROUGH OLD BOOKS, MAGAZINES, AND CATALOGUES. THEY GIVE HIM A SENSE OF WHAT THE WORLD WAS LIKE WHEN HIS BOOK IS SET.

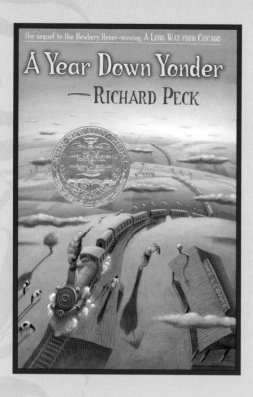

A Selected Bibliography of Peck's Work

Here Lies the Librarian (2006)

Teacher's Funeral: A Comedy in Three Parts (2004)

A River Between Us (2003)

A Year Down Yonder (2000)

London Holiday (1998)

A Long Way from Chicago: A Novel in Stories (1998)

Anonymously Yours (1995)

The Last Safe Place on Earth (1995)

Unfinished Portrait of Jessica (1991)

Princess Ashley (1987)

Remembering the Good Times (1985)

Representing Super Doll (1974)

Don't Look and It Won't Hurt (1971)

Peck's Major Literary Awards

2004 Scott O'Dell Award
  A River Between Us

2001 Newbery Medal
  A Year Down Yonder

1999 Newbery Honor Book
  A Long Way from Chicago: A Novel in Stories

readers will learn about independence, individuality, and self-confidence from his stories.

Many people wonder where Peck gets his ideas. His characters are so lifelike that they seem to be based on real people. A few of Peck's characters really are based on people he has known. Peck's great-uncle, for example, has a role in one of his books. But Peck usually uses his imagination to create his lively characters.

Peck's books have proved to be very popular. They have been

> *"I read because one life isn't enough, and in the pages of a book I can be anybody."*

translated into many different languages, and five of them have been made into movies. Peck has also received many awards for his writing. These honors include the Margaret A. Edwards Award, the Edgar Allen Poe Award, and the American Library Association's Young Adult Author Achievement Award. In 2001, Peck was awarded the greatest honor a children's author can receive. He won the Newbery Medal for *A Year Down Yonder.*

⌘

WHERE TO FIND OUT MORE ABOUT RICHARD PECK

BOOKS

Gallo, Donald R. *Presenting Richard Peck.* New York: Twayne, 1989.

McElmeel, Sharron L. *100 Most Popular Children's Authors: Biographical Sketches and Bibliographies.* Englewood, Colo.: Libraries Unlimited, 1999.

Peck, Richard. *Anonymously Yours.* New York: Beech Tree Books, 1995.

Silvey, Anita, ed. *The Essential Guide to Children's Books and Their Creators.* Boston: Houghton Mifflin Company, 2002.

WEB SITE

RICHARD PECK HOME PAGE
http://www.richardpeck.smartwriters.com/
For information about the author

———

PECK WRITES ALL OF HIS STORIES ON AN ELECTRIC TYPEWRITER. HE TRIED A COMPUTER FOR A WHILE, BUT DIDN'T LIKE IT.

Marcus Pfister

Born: July 30, 1960

Most of Marcus Pfister's books for children include animal characters. He believes that it is easier to tell a story using animals. "If I draw some houses or cities, they might look like European or American cities. An animal is an animal no matter where you are from. The penguin in America looks like a penguin in Japan," explains Pfister. He has written and illustrated more than twenty-five books for children. His best-known books include the Penguin Pete series, the Hopper series, and the Rainbow Fish series.

Marcus Pfister was born on July 30, 1960, in Bern, Switzerland. As a child, he was always interested in art. He wrote his own stories and painted pictures to go with them. Marcus also loved to listen to his father tell

PRODUCTS SUCH AS GAMES, PUZZLES, BUTTONS, AND FINGER PUPPETS HAVE BEEN CREATED FROM PFISTER'S RAINBOW FISH SERIES.

stories. "We didn't have a lot of children's books growing up, but my father always invented his own stories and told them to us," Pfister says.

When Marcus Pfister grew up, he decided to attend an art school in Bern. He also worked at an advertising agency. In 1981, he moved to Zurich, Switzerland, to work as a graphic designer. Pfister also spent time on his painting and other art. He was interested in illustrating a children's book, but he decided to improve his art skills before working on one.

A little later, Pfister and his wife took a six-month trip to the United States. When they returned to Switzerland, he decided to spend more time on

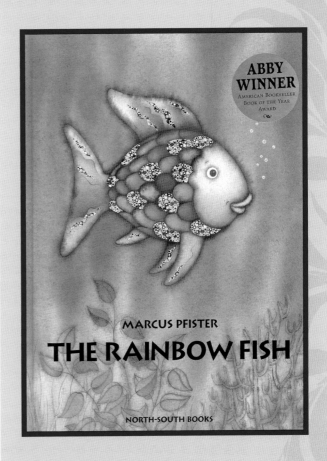

A Selected Bibliography of Pfister's Work

Holey Moley (2006)
Playtime with Rainbow Fish (2003)
Just the Way You Are (2002)
Rainbow Fish ABC (2002)
The Happy Hedgehog (2000)
How Leo Learned to Be King (1998)
Rainbow Fish and the Big Blue Whale (1998)
Penguin Pete (1997)
Milo and the Magical Stones (1997)
Rainbow Fish to the Rescue! (1995)
The Rainbow Fish (1992)
Hopper (Illustrations only, 1991)
The Sleepy Owl (1986)

his art. He worked part-time as a graphic designer and spent the rest of his time painting, sculpting, and creating a children's book.

The first book that Pfister wrote and illustrated was *The Sleepy Owl*. It was published in 1986. Most of Pfister's books are written in German and then translated into English.

Pfister's most popular books are in his Rainbow Fish series. The first Rainbow Fish book was published in 1992. More than 5 million copies have been sold throughout the world.

Pfister uses the fish character in the book to teach important lessons to children. He uses many of his books to teach children about sharing and the importance of friendship.

"The children I write the books for are often too young to read the stories themselves. So they need the parents to tell them the story. For me, it is most important that the parents and children come together, even if it is only for ten minutes in the evening."

Most of Pfister's illustrations are done with watercolor paints. He sometimes uses special techniques to make his pictures look just right. On pictures of his Rainbow Fish, Pfister uses foil stamping to make the illustration look shiny. He has won many awards for his Rainbow Fish illustrations.

PFISTER'S BOOKS HAVE BEEN TRANSLATED INTO MORE THAN THIRTY LANGUAGES, INCLUDING ENGLISH, CROATIAN, FRENCH, GREEK, KOREAN, AND THAI.

Pfister lives with his wife and three children in Bern. He continues to write and illustrate books for children.

❧

WHERE TO FIND OUT MORE ABOUT MARCUS PFISTER

BOOKS

Children's Literature Review. Vol. 42. Detroit: Gale Research, 1992.

Rockman, Connie C., ed. *Eighth Book of Junior Authors and Illustrators.* New York: H. W. Wilson Company, 2000.

WEB SITES

BRAVEMONSTER.COM
http://www.bravemonster.com/authors/marcuspfister.htm
To read a biography of Marcus Pfister

MARCUS PFISTER'S BOOKS
http://www.kiddyhouse.com/Teachers/Literature/Marcus.html
To find links to reviews of and activities related to Marcus Pfister's books

———

PFISTER'S BOOK *MILO AND THE MAGICAL STONES* HAS TWO DIFFERENT ENDINGS. ABOUT HALFWAY THROUGH THE BOOK, READERS CHOOSE WHETHER TO READ THE SAD ENDING OR THE HAPPY ENDING.

Rodman Philbrick

Born: 1951

Rodman Philbrick started writing when he was in the sixth grade. He wrote science fiction and short stories with trick endings like those used by the famous writer O. Henry and sent them to magazines such as *Amazing Stories* and the *New Yorker.* They were always rejected. When Rodman was sixteeen, he wrote his first novel, and over the next eleven years he wrote eight or nine more that were never published either.

Rodman Philbrick was born in 1951 in Boston, Massachusetts. He has lived near the New England seacoast most of his life. Philbrick attended the University of New Hampshire but dropped out to write. While he wrote his novels and collected his rejection slips, he worked as a longshoreman and built boats.

AS A CHILD, RODMAN PHILBRICK LIKED EDGAR RICE BURROUGHS'S TARZAN BOOKS AND THE JOHN CARTER OF MARS SERIES. HE ALSO LIKED COMIC BOOKS, MARK TWAIN, *A WRINKLE IN TIME,* AND *THE PHANTOM TOLLBOOTH.*

At the time he wrote genre stories. "No experimental flourishes," he says. "No illusions about great literature." At the age of twenty-seven, he published his first book, *Shooting Star,* a mystery for adults. Philbrick wrote more mysteries, some of them as W. R. Philbrick, and some under the pen name William R. Dantz.

An editor asked Philbrick if he'd like to write a mystery for children. Philbrick said he would try. But on the way home from the meeting, something odd happened. "This young voice suddenly comes into my head," Philbrick explains, "and the first thing he says is: 'I never had a brain until Freak came along and let me borrow his for a while, and that's the truth, the whole truth.' " Without intending to, Philbrick had begun *Freak the Mighty.*

Freak was inspired by a boy who lived near Philbrick, the son of one of his friends. The boy had Morquio syndrome, which meant that he would never grow to be more than three feet tall, and he suffered from many medical problems. He was very intelligent and loved words and books. Philbrick

> *"When I started writing stories in the sixth grade . . . it was something I felt I should do secretly. Writing wasn't cool, like being good at sports, or being part of the in crowd. . . . Writing wasn't a 'normal' activity, and like most kids that age, I desperately wanted to be 'normal.'"*

PHILBRICK'S PASSION IS FISHING. HE WRITES EVERY MORNING AND FISHES IN THE AFTERNOON. HE HAS THREE BOATS, AND HE ESTIMATES THAT HE FISHES **300** DAYS EACH YEAR.

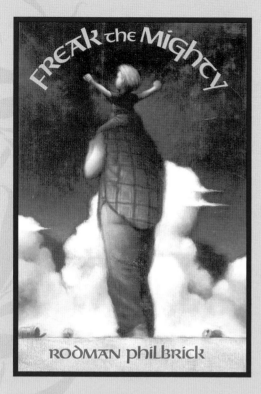

A Selected Bibliography of Philbrick's Work

The Young Man and the Sea (2004)
Coffins (2002)
The Last Book in the Universe (2000)
REM World (2000)
Max the Mighty (1998)
Strange Invaders (1997)
Children of the Wolf (1996)
The Fire Pony (1996)
Night Creature (1996)
The Wereing (1996)
The Horror (1995)
Freak the Mighty (1993)

used to see him being carried down the street on another boy's back. That image—of two boys walking as one—became the starting point for *Freak the Mighty*. The novel is about one boy with intelligence and not much strength, and another boy with strength and not much intelligence.

Freak took less than two months to write. It was published in 1993 and was made into a movie.

Philbrick wrote more novels for young adults. In *The Fire Pony*, a boy gets a palomino pony ready for a rodeo while worrying about his brother, who has a history of arson. *Max the Mighty* is a sequel to *Freak*. This time

Max, the strong boy from *Freak,* helps

Worm, a girl from an abusive family.

Philbrick has also started several

paperback horror and science-fiction

series for young readers, writing some

of them with his wife, Lynn Harnett.

Two of his recent books for young

"I'm not worried about the future of books. I've published a novel for adults in electronic format and expect that I will be doing so for my younger readers in the near future."

adults, *The Last Book in the Universe* and *REM World,* are science fiction.

He continues to write for adults, too. Philbrick and his wife live in

Maine and the Florida Keys.

WHERE TO FIND OUT MORE ABOUT RODMAN PHILBRICK

BOOKS
Authors and Artists for Young Adults.
Vol. 31. Detroit: Gale Research, 1999.

Rockman, Connie C., ed. *The Ninth Book of Junior Authors and Illustrators.*
New York: H. W. Wilson Company, 2004.

WEB SITES
RODMAN PHILBRICK HOME PAGE
http://www.rodmanphilbrick.com/
To read information about Rodman Philbrick's life and books

SCHOLASTIC ONLINE ACTIVITIES
http://teacher.scholastic.com/writewit/bookrev/index.htm
To read Rodman Philbrick's biography and writing tips

WHEN RODMAN PHILBRICK WROTE HIS FIRST STORIES IN THE SIXTH GRADE, HE KEPT THEM SECRET FROM HIS FRIENDS AND FAMILY. HE SENT HANDWRITTEN PAGES TO A TYPING SERVICE ADVERTISED IN A COMIC BOOK.

Dav Pilkey

Born: March 4, 1966

Kids love him! He is Captain Underpants. He flies around the city in his underwear. But he is only make-believe. He is created by children's author Dav Pilkey. Pilkey is the popular author and illustrator of many children's books, including the Captain Underpants and Dumb Bunnies series.

Dav Pilkey was born on March 4, 1966, in Cleveland, Ohio. As a child, Dav always loved to draw. "When I wasn't laughing, I kept myself busy drawing. While the other kids in the neighborhood were outside playing baseball and football, I was inside drawing animals, monsters, and super-hero guys," Pilkey remembers.

DAV USED TO BE SPELLED *DAVE.* THEY LEFT THE *E* OFF
HIS NAME TAG WHEN HE WORKED AT PIZZA HUT, AND HE LIKED IT!

He attended St. John's Lutheran School in Elyria, Ohio. School was not a fun place for Dav. He had a reading disability and was hyperactive. But his teachers and parents did not realize that at first. Learning to read and paying attention were hard. Today, the characters in Pilkey's books struggle with the same problems.

In school, Dav was the class clown. He got in trouble almost every day for his behavior. He was often sent out of class to the hall. While sitting in the hall, Dav would draw. He would staple sheets of paper together and make his own books. His friends loved his books. His teachers did not. They were silly—about a man flying around in his underwear!

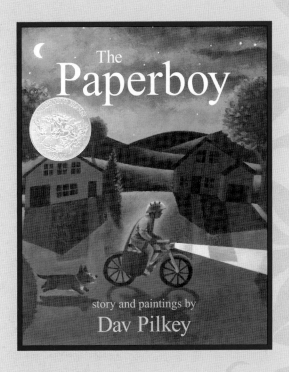

A Selected Bibliography of Pilkey's Work

Ricky Ricotta's Mighty Robot vs. the Uranium Unicorn from Uranus (2005)

The Complete Adventures of Big Dog and Little Dog (2003)

The Adventures of Super Diaper Baby (2002)

Ricky Ricotta's Giant Robot: An Epic Novel (2000)

The Adventures of Captain Underpants: An Epic Novel (1997)

The Dumb Bunnies Go to the Zoo (Illustrations only, 1997)

Make Way for Dumb Bunnies (Illustrations only, 1996)

The Paperboy (1996)

The Dumb Bunnies (Illustrations only, 1994)

Dragon's Halloween: Dragon's Fifth Tale (1993)

Kat Kong: Starring Flash, Rabies, and Dwayne and Introducing Blueberry As the Monster (1993)

Dragon's Fat Cat: Dragon's Fourth Tale (1992)

When Cats Dream (1992)

A Friend for Dragon (1991)

Pilkey's Major Literary Awards

1997 Caldecott Honor Book
  The Paperboy

> *"When I really got serious about writing children's books, I began reading everything I could by my favorite writers. . . . Soon I began to see what really worked in these books—what made them great pieces of literature."*

After high school, Pilkey wanted to study art. He went to Kent State University in Ohio. An English teacher there encouraged him to write stories. Pilkey began working on a children's book. He entered it in a writing contest called National Written and Illustrated by . . . Awards Contest for Students. He won! That was the start of his career as a children's book author and illustrator.

There are now almost forty books that Pilkey has written, illustrated, or both. The Captain Underpants series has been published in seventeen different languages. The characters in the series, George and Harold, are much like Pilkey was as a boy. They don't fit in with all the other kids in school. "Being a kid can be pretty tough sometimes, and being different will almost always get you in trouble with everybody else who is desperately trying to fit in. But being different is a good thing," Pilkey states.

Pilkey writes books that he would have liked to have read as a child. He writes about animals. He uses pictures to help the words tell a story. His stories are funny. He has said that he never has to work to think of

PILKEY USES THE PEN NAME SUE DENIM WHEN HE
WORKS ON THE DUMB BUNNIES BOOKS.

an idea for a story. The ideas just come to him. Pilkey likes to spend time doing quiet things. "I love to watch the sun set, listen to the rain, walk my dog, and sit in front of the fire. It is usually then, when I am quiet and at rest, that my ideas come to me," he says.

Dav Pilkey now lives in Eugene, Oregon, with his many pets. He continues to write his popular stories for children.

❧

WHERE TO FIND OUT MORE ABOUT DAV PILKEY

BOOKS

Hedblad, Alan, ed. *Something about the Author.*
Vol. 68. Detroit: Gale Research, 1992.

Holtze, Sally Holmes, ed. *Seventh Book of Junior Authors & Illustrators.*
New York: H. W. Wilson Company, 1996.

WEB SITES

DAV PILKEY'S WEB SITE O' FUN!
http://www.pilkey.com/
To get information about Dav Pilkey

EDUCATIONAL PAPERBACK ASSOCIATION
http://edupaperback.org/showauth.cfm?authid=245
To read about the Dav Pilkey's life and work

PILKEY GETS MORE THAN **1,000** FAN LETTERS EACH WEEK.

Brian Pinkney

Born: August 28, 1961

From the start of his career, Brian Pinkney had a goal. He wanted to create, and he has been successful. Pinkney has received many honors and awards for his moving illustrations of African American characters.

Brian Pinkney was born on August 28, 1961, in Boston, Massachusetts. Growing up, Brian, his sister, and his two brothers were surrounded by music, art, and books. Their father, Jerry Pinkney, is an award-winning children's book illustrator. Their mother, Gloria Jean Pinkney, is a noted children's book author. These artistic parents made sure that their children were occupied with one creative activity after another.

When Brian was young, his teachers encouraged his love of art. Although they didn't want him to doodle on his papers, many teachers allowed Brian to create posters for extra credit. After school, Brian

WHEN HE WAS YOUNG, BRIAN PINKNEY ADMIRED LEONARDO DA VINCI. WHEN HE READ THAT LEONARDO WROTE BACKWARD, PINKNEY BEGAN WRITING HIS CLASS NOTES THE SAME WAY. UNFORTUNATELY, HE HAD TO HOLD THEM UP TO A MIRROR TO STUDY!

would visit his father's studio. There, he watched his father work. Brian paid careful attention to his father's techniques. Then he would go back to his own little studio in a walk-in closet and try the techniques himself.

> *"I make pictures for the child in me. My work is actually my way of playing. That's why I think children enjoy my books; they recognize me as one of their own."*

After he graduated from high school, Pinkney enrolled in the Philadelphia College of Art to find out as much as he could about drawing and painting. Then he went to the School of Visual Arts in New York City to learn even more. There, Pinkney was introduced to medium he would become known for: scratchboard. A scratchboard is a white board that is covered with black ink. Pinkney scratches his drawings into the ink with a sharp tool, etching the ink to expose the white area underneath. Finally, he uses watercolors, oil paints, or acrylic paints to add color and life to his etchings.

Pinkney's specialty is African American themes. He loves sharing little-known facts about African American history, folklore, and culture. Pinkney has illustrated books about famous African Americans Benjamin Banneker, Alvin Ailey, Bill Pickett, and Duke Ellington.

Pinkney has illustrated books by many children's authors, but his favorite coworker is his wife, Andrea Davis Pinkney. The couple have

PINKNEY LIKES TO LISTEN TO MUSIC WHILE HE DRAWS—EVERYTHING FROM CLASSICAL TO RAP. WHILE ILLUSTRATING A BOOK ABOUT DUKE ELLINGTON, PINKNEY PLAYED ELLINGTON'S MUSIC.

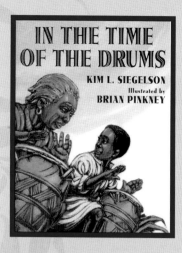

A Selected Bibliography of Pinkney's Work

Peggony Po: A Whale of a Tale (Illustration only, 2006)

Hush, Little Baby (2006)

Sleeping Cutie (Illustrations only, 2004)

Jackie's Bat (Illustrations only, 2003)

Cosmo and the Robot (2000)

In the Time of the Drums (Illustrations only, 1999)

Cendrillon: A Caribbean Cinderella (Illustrations only, 1998)

Duke Ellington: The Piano Prince and His Orchestra (Illustrations only, 1998)

The Adventures of Sparrowboy (1997)

I Smell Honey (1997)

Watch Me Dance (1997)

Faithful Friend (Illustrations only, 1995)

Max Found Two Sticks (1994)

Happy Birthday, Martin Luther King (Illustrations only, 1993)

Sukey and the Mermaid (Illustrations only, 1992)

The Ballad of Belle Dorcas (Illustrations only, 1990)

The Boy and the Ghost (Illustrations only, 1989)

Pinkney's Major Literary Awards

2000 Coretta Scott King Illustrator Award
   In the Time of the Drums

1999 Caldecott Honor Book
1999 Coretta Scott King Illustrator Honor Book
   Duke Ellington: The Piano Prince and His Orchestra

1997 Boston Globe–Horn Book Picture Book Award
   The Adventures of Sparrowboy

1996 Caldecott Honor Book
1996 Coretta Scott King Illustrator Honor Book
   Faithful Friend

1993 Coretta Scott King Illustrator Honor Book
   Sukey and the Mermaid

created many great children's books together. One, *Duke Ellington: The Piano Prince and His Orchestra,* was named a Caldecott Honor Book.

Pinkney also illustrates books that he writes himself. He gets his ideas from childhood experiences and from his imagination. The idea for *The Adventures of Sparrowboy* came to him while he was riding the subway. This fun fantasy book, illustrated in comic-book style, is about a boy who is granted the ability to fly—by a bird!

In addition to creating children's books, Pinkney also contributes art to adult magazines. His work has appeared in the *New York Times Magazine,*

Ebony, Women's Day, and *Instructor.* Exhibits of Pinkney's artwork have appeared around the country.

Today Pinkney, his wife, and their daughter live in Brooklyn, New York. When Pinkney isn't illustrating books or teaching art, he likes to play the drums. He also likes to visit elementary schools and talk to students about art and his books.

> *"I want to put forth positive images of African American people in portraits that are truthful and beautiful."*

WHERE TO FIND OUT MORE ABOUT BRIAN PINKNEY

BOOKS

Cummings, Pat, ed. *Talking with Artists, Vol. 2: Conversations with Thomas B. Allen, Mary Jane Begin, Floyd Cooper, Julie Downing, Denise Fleming, Sheila Hamanaka, Kevin Henkes, William Joyce, Maira Kalman, Deborah Nourse Lattimore, Brian Pinkney, Vera B. Williams and David Wisniewski.* New York: Simon & Schuster, 1995.

Kovacs, Deborah, and James Preller. *Meet the Authors and Illustrators: 60 Creators of Favorite Children's Books Talk about Their Work.* Vol. 2. New York: Scholastic, 1993.

WEB SITE

HOUGHTON MIFFLIN READING
http://www.eduplace.com/kids/hmr/mtai/bpinkney.html
To meet Brian Pinkney

AS A CHILD, BRIAN PINKNEY AND HIS SIBLINGS SOMETIMES SERVED AS MODELS FOR THEIR FATHER'S ART. IN 1989, THE TABLES WERE TURNED. PINKNEY USED HIS DAD AS A MODEL FOR HIS BOOK *THE BOY AND THE GHOST.*

Jerry Pinkney

Born: December 22, 1939

An interest in a variety of cultures is an important part of Jerry Pinkney's art. Pinkney gets a great deal of inspiration from African American culture. He is proud of his heritage and wants to be a role model for other African Americans. Pinkney has been illustrating books for children and young people for more than thirty-five years. He has illustrated more than eighty books written by other authors. His most popular books include *Uncle Remus: The Complete Tales; John Henry;* and *Sam and the Tigers: A New Telling of Little Black Sambo.*

Jerry Pinkney was born on December 22, 1939, in Philadelphia, Pennsylvania. He became interested in drawing at a young age. At first, he would draw to copy his older brothers, who drew pictures from magazines and comic books. Jerry

PINKNEY'S ARTWORK AND ILLUSTRATIONS HAVE BEEN EXHIBITED AT MANY SHOWS IN THE UNITED STATES, JAPAN, AND ITALY.

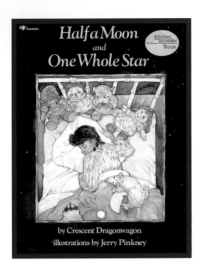

Half a Moon and One Whole Star
by Crescent Dragonwagon
illustrations by Jerry Pinkney

soon discovered that he really enjoyed drawing. He spent much of his time drawing and working on his art.

Jerry knew that he wanted to study to be an artist. His mother was very supportive. She wanted to help him be successful at whatever he wanted to do. Jerry's father was not sure about his son becoming an artist. Eventually, though, he understood that Jerry loved drawing and could be a great artist.

A Selected Bibliography of Pinkney's Work

Little Red Hen (2006)

God Bless the Child (Illustrations only, 2004)

Noah's Ark (2002)

The Nightingale (2002)

Goin' Someplace Special (Illustrations only, 2000)

The Ugly Duckling (Illustrations only, 1999)

Uncle Remus: The Complete Tales (Illustrations only, 1999)

Minty: A Story of Young Harriet Tubman (Illustrations only, 1996)

John Henry (Illustrations only, 1994)

The Talking Eggs: A Folktale from the American South (Illustrations only, 1989)

Mirandy and Brother Wind (Illustrations only, 1988)

Half a Moon and One Whole Star (Illustrations only, 1986)

The Patchwork Quilt (Illustrations only, 1985)

Childtimes: A Three-Generation Memoir (Illustrations only, 1979)

The Adventures of Spider: West African Folk Tales (Illustrations only, 1964)

Pinkney's Major Literary Awards

2005 Coretta Scott King Illustrator Honor Book
  God Bless the Child

2003 Caldecott Honor Book
  Noah's Ark

2002 Coretta Scott King Illustrator Award
  Goin' Someplace Special

2000 Caldecott Honor Book
  The Ugly Duckling

1997 Coretta Scott King Illustrator Award
  Minty: A Story of Young Harriet Tubman

1995 Boston Globe–Horn Book Picture Book Award
1995 Caldecott Honor Book
  John Henry

1990 Caldecott Honor Book
1990 Coretta Scott King Illustrator Honor Book
  The Talking Eggs: A Folktale from the American South

1989 Caldecott Honor Book
1989 Coretta Scott King Illustrator Award
  Mirandy and Brother Wind

1987 Coretta Scott King Illustrator Award
  Half a Moon and One Whole Star

1986 Coretta Scott King Illustrator Award
  The Patchwork Quilt

1981 Coretta Scott King Illustrator Honor Book
  Count on Your Fingers African Style

1980 Boston Globe–Horn Book Nonfiction Honor Book
  Childtimes: A Three-Generation Memoir

"*I don't see things until I draw them. When I put a line down, I know how it should feel, and I know when it doesn't feel right. I work with a pencil in one hand and an eraser in the other, not knowing what I have until I put it down.*"

When he was a teenager, Jerry sold newspapers at a newsstand. He would bring his sketch pad with him to work. He drew pictures of the people and scenes he saw on the street. A professional cartoonist who stopped at Jerry's newsstand almost every day noticed Jerry's drawings and invited him to his art studio. The cartoonist and Jerry became good friends, and Jerry learned that he could make a living as an artist.

After finishing a commercial art course, Pinkney received a scholarship to attend classes at the Philadelphia Museum of Art. He met and married his wife, Gloria, while attending school. When he graduated, Pinkney and his wife moved to Boston. He worked as an illustrator for a greeting card company. He gained a great reputation as an illustrator and opened a graphic design studio with two other artists. Pinkney later opened his own studio when he moved to New York.

Pinkney creates art and illustrations for many purposes. He enjoys illustrating children's books. "Books give me a great feeling of personal and artistic satisfaction," Pinkney says. "When I'm working on a book I

PINKNEY CREATED THE ILLUSTRATIONS FOR A SET OF POSTAGE STAMPS FOR THE BLACK HERITAGE SERIES FOR THE U.S. POSTAL SERVICE.

wish the phone would never ring. I love doing it. My satisfaction comes from the actual marks on the paper, and when it sings, it's magic."

Pinkney lives in Westchester County, New York, with his wife. He has also been an art professor and still gives workshops throughout the country. He continues to create illustrations for books along with his other works of art.

> *"The marriage of typography and illustration was always very important to me, and the picture-book area provided me with the opportunity to illustrate and design."*

&

WHERE TO FIND OUT MORE ABOUT JERRY PINKNEY

BOOKS

Kovacs, Deborah, and James Preller. *Meet the Authors and Illustrators: 60 Creators of Favorite Children's Books Talk about Their Work.* Vol. 1. New York: Scholastic, 1991.

McElmeel, Sharron L. *100 Most Popular Picture Book Authors and Illustrators: Biographical Sketches and Bibliographies.* Englewood, Colo.: Libraries Unlimited, 2000.

WEB SITES

BOOK PAGE
http://www.bookpage.com/0402bp/meet_jerry_pinkney.html
For an interview of Jerry Pinkney

HOUGHTON MIFFLIN READING
http://www.eduplace.com/kids/hmr/mtai/jpinkney.html
To meet Jerry Pinkney

PINKNEY'S WIFE, GLORIA, IS AN AUTHOR AND ILLUSTRATOR OF CHILDREN'S BOOKS. HE HAS CREATED ILLUSTRATIONS FOR SOME OF HER BOOKS. HIS SON BRIAN IS ALSO AN AWARD-WINNING ILLUSTRATOR AND ARTIST.

Daniel Manus Pinkwater

Born: November 15, 1941

trange things happen in Daniel Manus Pinkwater's books. A boy discovers that giant lizards are making music on his television late at night. A 266-pound chicken named Henrietta terrorizes the quiet city of Hoboken, New Jersey. An elderly relative arrives for a visit, only to reveal that he is actually an intergalactic space traveler. Fat men from space, with thick eyeglasses and identical plaid sport coats, try to steal all the earth's junk food. Pinkwater's books are filled with wild events and silly jokes, along with a sprinkling of serious ideas and references to great artists.

Daniel Manus Pinkwater was born on November 15, 1941, in Memphis, Tennessee. He spent most of his youth in Chicago. Daniel and

PINKWATER AND HIS WIFE, JILL, HAVE WORKED AS PROFESSIONAL DOG TRAINERS. THEY LEARNED TO TRAIN DOGS AFTER BUYING A POORLY BEHAVED MALAMUTE PUPPY. JILL HAS ALSO ILLUSTRATED A NUMBER OF PINKWATER'S BOOKS.

his friends used to act out adventure stories they had read—like *20,000 Leagues under the Sea* and *The Three Musketeers.*

Chicago appears in many of Pinkwater's books—sometimes called Hogboro, and sometimes Baconburg. Local landmarks turn up in his stories with more or less new names (for example, the Newberry Library becomes the Blueberry Library in the Snarkout Boys novels). One legendary Chicago character, an old man who used to ride the city's buses with a trained chicken, turns up in several Pinkwater books. In *Lizard Music,* he is a key to the secret of the lizards.

> *"When I was a student I invented a number of practices that, I vaguely hoped, would help me become a good artist. . . . The first thing I did was teach myself to sit at a table. Seems simple, but not many people can do it."*

Pinkwater attended Bard College in New York and then moved to New York City. He wanted to be a sculptor and has worked as an art teacher at settlement houses. He didn't intend to write children's books. He got started almost by accident, when he ended up writing a book that he had been hired to illustrate.

Pinkwater has written about eighty books for children. Some of the best-known are *Lizard Music, The Last Guru, Fat Men from Space,* and *The Wuggie Norple Story.* In *The Wuggie Norple Story,* a man named Lunchbox Louie brings home a series of unlikely pets. Most of the fun comes from

---

FOOD PLAYS A BIG ROLE IN PINKWATER'S BOOKS. *SLAVES OF SPIEGEL* IS ABOUT AN INTERGALACTIC JUNK-FOOD CONTEST THAT INCLUDES A DESSERT MADE FROM EGGPLANT, PIZZA DOUGH, ICE CREAM, FIGS, PISTACHIOS, AND LOBSTER.

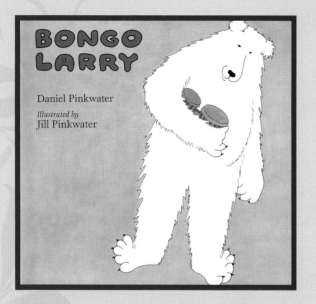

BONGO LARRY

Daniel Pinkwater

Illustrated by
Jill Pinkwater

A Selected Bibliography of Pinkwater's Work

Bad Bear Detectives (2006)
Artsy Smartsy Club (2005)
Looking for Bobowicz: A Hoboken Chicken Story (2004)
The Picture of Morty and Ray (2003)
Cone Kong: The Scary Ice Cream Giant (2001)
Irving and Muktuk: Two Bad Bears (2001)
The Magic Pretzel (2000)
Bongo Larry (1998)
At the Hotel Larry (1997)
Borgel (1990)
The Moosepire (1986)
The Muffin Fiend (1986)
Jolly Roger, a Dog of Hoboken (1985)
Devil in the Drain (1984)
Ducks! (1984)
Roger's Umbrella (1982)
Slaves of Spiegel (1982)
Young Adult Novel (1982)
The Worms of Kukumlima (1981)
Tooth-Gnasher Superflash (1981)
The Magic Moscow (1980)
The Wuggie Norple Story (1980)
Return of the Moose (1979)
The Last Guru (1978)
Fat Men from Space (1977)
Lizard Music (1976)

the names of the animals and the other characters: Exploding Pop Tart, Papercup Mixmaster, Bigfoot the Chipmunk, and, of course, Wuggie Norple himself.

Many of Pinkwater's stories borrow characters and plots from classic science fiction and horror books and movies, but they usually add a new twist. Instead of Frankenstein's monster, Pinkwater has the Frankenbagel (which, fortunately, gets stale just as it is about to attack). His werewolves attend school, and

"Here's my policy regarding experts in creative writing: Ignore what they say. . . . It might be a good idea to ignore what I say too. May as well be thorough."

they can be cured by eating a magic pretzel. Instead of vampires, he has "wempires," who don't drink blood, but wear plaid pants and talk with Yiddish accents. Pinkwater's heroes are often misfits and outsiders who have wonderful experiences because they are open to them.

Daniel Manus Pinkwater has also written magazine articles and books for adults. Since the 1980s, he has been a commentator on National Public Radio, talking about books, art, dogs, and—most of all—his life.

❧

WHERE TO FIND OUT MORE ABOUT DANIEL MANUS PINKWATER

BOOKS

Hogan, Walter. *The Agony and the Eggplant.* Lanham, Md.: Scarecrow Press, 2001.

Kovacs, Deborah, and James Preller. *Meet the Authors and Illustrators: 60 Creators of Favorite Children's Books Talk about Their Work.* Vol. 2. New York: Scholastic, 1993.

Pinkwater, Daniel Manus. *Chicago Days/Hoboken Nights.* Reading, Mass.: Addison-Wesley, 1991.

Silvey, Anita, ed. *The Essential Guide to Children's Books and Their Creators.* Boston: Houghton Mifflin Company, 2002.

WEB SITES

KIDSPACE
http://www.ipl.org/div/kidspace/askauthor/Pinkwater.html
To read an interview with Daniel Pinkwater

THE OFFICIAL PINKWATER SITE
http://www.pinkwater.com/indexh.html
To get information about Daniel Pinkwater, with links

———

ONE OF PINKWATER'S RECENT PROJECTS IS *CHINWAG THEATER,* A RADIO PROGRAM ON NATIONAL PUBLIC RADIO THAT FEATURES STORIES AND MUSIC.

Patricia Polacco

Born: July 11, 1944

I n her picture books, Patricia Polacco returns again and again to stories from her family and stories about the ethnic groups that make up the United States. Polacco herself has experienced many cultures. Her father's family came from Ireland, and her mother's family is from Russia. Her best friend when she was growing up was African American, and her husband is an Italian Jew who survived the Holocaust in Europe.

Patricia Polacco was born on July 11, 1944, in Lansing, Michigan. Her parents divorced when she was three years old, and she and her brother spent school years with their mother and summers with their father. Some of the time they lived on a farm in Michigan with their grandmother. After Patricia's grandmother died, the family moved to Florida and then to California.

Patricia grew up surrounded by storytellers, and she says that is how she learned the varied voices in her

POLACCO WRITES BOOKS WHILE SITTING IN ONE OF HER TWELVE ROCKING CHAIRS. SHE KEEPS A PAD OF PAPER BY EACH CHAIR SO SHE CAN JOT DOWN IDEAS.

books. "From my Russian background my stories are kind of ethnic, primitive, Eastern European—that's one type of voice I write in," she says. "Another is my midwestern American farm voice. I also write in a Jewish voice—my family was part Jewish and part Christian, which is an amazing thing. I write in all of the above, all of those voices because they more or less have been the places that I've lived."

Patricia had a hard time in school. She had dyslexia, which made it hard for her to read and write. Her book *Thank You, Mr. Falker* tells the story of how she finally got help from a teacher who realized what the problem was. Patricia was skillful at drawing, though.

A Selected Bibliography of Polacco's Work

Rotten Richie and the Ultimate Dare (2006)
Emma Kate (2005)
Orange for Frankie (2004)
G Is for Goat (2003)
When Lightning Comes in a Jar (2002)
Betty Doll (2001)
Mr. Lincoln's Way (2001)
The Butterfly (2000)
Welcome Comfort (1999)
Thank You, Mr. Falker (1998)
In Enzo's Splendid Gardens (1997)
I Can Hear the Sun: A Modern Myth (1996)
Firetalking (1994)
The Bee Tree (1993)
Chicken Sunday (1992)
Mrs. Katz and Tush (1992)
Some Birthday! (1991)
Babushka's Doll (1990)
Just Plain Fancy (1990)
Thunder Cake (1990)
Uncle Vova's Tree (1989)
The Keeping Quilt (1988)
Rechenka's Eggs (1988)
Meteor! (1987)

> *"I come from a family of storytellers, and when you're raised by people who tell, you're doomed. You're going to be a teller. . . . You embroider things and love to watch someone's face and see if they're going to react. If they do, you start adding stuff to make a good story."*

Polacco won a scholarship to college, but she decided to get married instead. When the marriage ended in divorce, she returned to school, first in California, and then in Australia. She studied Russian and Greek art and earned a Ph.D. degree.

Polacco had always made books of drawings for friends. When she was about forty years old, she joined a group of writers and illustrators and learned how to turn her ideas into children's books. She went to New York City with an eighty-pound portfolio of samples and book "dummies" (rough-draft books that show how the words and pictures fit together on the page). She visited sixteen publishers in a week and sold her first book, *Meteor!*

Meteor! was based on a story Polacco heard from her family. It tells the tale of what happens on a little farm in Michigan after a meteorite falls there.

More books followed—more than thirty in all. *Rechenka's Eggs* is about Ukrainian Easter egg painting. *The Keeping Quilt* tells about her Russian great-grandmother, who made a quilt of clothes she had worn

POLACCO HAS THE QUILT SHE WROTE ABOUT IN *THE KEEPING QUILT*.
WHEN SHE WAS A GIRL, IT COVERED HER BED, AND HER GRANDMOTHER
USED TO TELL HER STORIES ABOUT THE MEMORIES SEWED INTO IT.

in the old country to help her remember it. In *Chicken Sunday,* African American and white children try to buy Miss Eula a new hat and become friends with a Jewish shopkeeper.

Patricia Polacco has two grown children. She likes to visit schools to promote reading, and she started an organization that tries to stop bullying.

> *"My thoughts boil in my head. They catch the air and fly. The images and stories come back with fury and energy. . . . My heart sings whenever I am drawing."*

WHERE TO FIND OUT MORE ABOUT PATRICIA POLACCO

BOOKS

Kovacs, Deborah, and James Preller. *Meet the Authors and Illustrators: 60 Creators of Favorite Children's Books Talk about Their Work.* Vol. 2. New York: Scholastic, 1993.

McElmeel, Sharron L. *100 Most Popular Children's Authors: Biographical Sketches and Bibliographies.* Englewood, Colo.: Libraries Unlimited, 1999.

Polacco, Patricia. *Firetalking.* Katonah, N.Y.: R. C. Owen, 1994.

WEB SITES

EDUCATIONAL PAPERBACK ASSOCIATION
http://edupaperback.org/showauth.cfm?authid=39
To read about Patricia Polacco's life and work

PATRICIA POLACCO HOME PAGE
http://www.patriciapolacco.com/
To read news and information about Patricia Polacco

BEFORE SHE WROTE CHILDREN'S BOOKS, POLACCO WORKED FOR MUSEUMS, HELPING TO PRESERVE AND RESTORE VALUABLE OLD RELIGIOUS PAINTINGS (OR ICONS) FROM RUSSIA AND GREECE.

Leo Politi

Born: November 21, 1908
Died: March 24, 1996

Leo Politi's illustrated stories are considered modern classics. Politi is best known for portraying children in the many multicultural neighborhoods of Los Angeles, California. Many of his books highlight the vibrant Hispanic neighborhood around Olvera Street.

Leo Politi was born in 1908 in Fresno, California. Both his parents were immigrants from Italy. Leo spent the first few years of his life on a ranch near Fresno, where his father worked as a buyer and seller of horses.

When Leo was seven, the family moved back to his mother's hometown of Broni, in northern Italy. Leo enjoyed a happy childhood there, and he drew pictures constantly. At age fifteen, he won a scholarship to study at the National Art Institute in Monza, near Milan. There he studied drawing, design, architecture, and sculpture. After six years of study, he was qualified to be an art teacher. However, he spent time designing textiles and tapestries instead.

POLITI PAINTED THE MURAL "THE BLESSING OF THE ANIMALS" ON THE BISCAILUZ BUILDING ON LOS ANGELES'S OLVERA STREET. IT DEPICTS AN ANNUAL NEIGHBORHOOD EVENT IN WHICH A LOCAL PRIEST BLESSES NEIGHBORHOOD CATS AND DOGS.

At age twenty-two, Politi sailed back to the United States. His route took him through the Panama Canal and up the Pacific coast. On the way, he had a chance to visit several Latin American countries. He admired the people he met there. Back in Fresno, Politi met Helen Fontes, and they were soon

"I had always drawn [the Little Pancho character] for fun, and one night I started to draw him running and he ran all over the page and right into his own story."

married. The couple settled in the Bunker Hill section of Los Angeles. In time, their family grew to include two children, Paul and Suzanne.

At first, Politi tried to earn a living as a street artist. He set up his easel and paints in front of a café on Olvera Street. Sometimes he painted tourists' portraits. At other times, he painted whatever he saw—Hispanics playing music, women making tortillas, and kids frolicking in the street.

"Sometimes, with just a knife, I carved on discarded blocks of wood I found [on Olvera Street]."

Often, his wife sat beside him as he worked. "And many a cold night," he recalled, "we waited for customers who never came."

Eventually, Politi began drawing illustrations for the

WHEN POLITI AUTOGRAPHED A BOOK, HE OFTEN SKETCHED
A BIRD OR FLOWER ALONG WITH HIS SIGNATURE.

A Selected Bibliography of Politi's Work

Mr. Fong's Toy Shop (1978)

Three Stalks of Corn (1976)

Mieko (1969)

Rosa (1963)

Moy Moy (1960)

The Butterflies Come (1957)

The Mission Bell (1953)

Looking-for-Something: The Story of a Stray Burro in Ecuador (Illustrations only, 1952)

Little Leo (1951)

At the Palace Gates (Illustrations only, 1949)

Song of the Swallows (1949)

Juanita (1948)

Pedro, the Angel of Olvera Street (1946)

Little Pancho (1938)

Politi's Major Literary Awards

1952 Caldecott Medal
 Song of the Swallows

1949 Caldecott Honor Book
 Juanita

1947 Caldecott Honor Book
 Pedro, the Angel of Olvera Street

magazine *Script*. One of the characters he drew reappeared in his book *Little Pancho*, published in 1938. It was the first book that Politi wrote and illustrated.

Over the next few years, Politi illustrated several books written by other authors. One year, he painted a series of Christmas cards and sent them to book editors. An editor at Scribner's was impressed by Politi's work and encouraged him to write and illustrate another book. He did, and *Pedro, the Angel of Olvera Street* was published in 1946. It depicted children he had drawn for those Christmas cards.

One of Politi's most popular books is *Song of the*

Swallows. It tells about the swallows that return to California's San Juan de Capistrano Mission every spring. His book *Little Leo* tells the story of his own childhood journey from California to Italy. Other books depict children in Los Angeles's Chinese and Japanese neighborhoods, as well as the Olvera Street area.

Leo Politi died in Los Angeles at the age of eighty-seven.

❧

WHERE TO FIND OUT MORE ABOUT LEO POLITI

BOOKS

Silvey, Anita, ed. *The Essential Guide to Children's Books and Their Creators.* Boston: Houghton Mifflin Company, 2002.

Stalcup, Ann. *Leo Politi: Artist of the Angels.* New York: Silver Moon Press, 2004.

WEB SITES

ENCYCLOPEDIA BRITANNICA
http://www.britannica.com/ebi/article-9333432
For a biography with a listing of his major works

THE HORN BOOK VIRTUAL HISTORY EXHIBIT
http://www.hbook.com/exhibit/politibio.html
For a biography of Leo Politi

AN ELEMENTARY SCHOOL IN WEST LOS ANGELES IS NAMED AFTER POLITI.

Beatrix Potter

Born: July 28, 1866
Died: December 22, 1943

In 1893, Beatrix Potter sat down to write a letter to a sick five-year-old. "My dear Noel," she began, "I don't know what to write to you, so I shall tell you a story about four little rabbits." A few years later, this story became *The Tale of Peter Rabbit.* Potter's tale about the adventures of Flopsy, Mopsy, Cotton-tail, and Peter would become one of the world's most famous children's books. And Beatrix Potter would become one of the world's best-loved children's authors.

Beatrix Potter was born on July 28, 1866, in London, England. Her wealthy family lived in a large house, but she was a lonely child. Rather than going to school, she was educated at home by a governess.

POTTER ACTUALLY HAD A PET RABBIT NAMED PETER.

Beatrix's parents were very protective of Beatrix and her younger brother, Bertram. The two seldom saw other children. Instead, they made friends with animals and collected all sorts of creatures, including a rabbit, a snake, a tortoise, two lizards, a frog, and some newts. Beatrix made careful drawings of her pets.

During the summers, the Potters vacationed in Scotland or in the Lake District of northern England. There, Beatrix was allowed all the freedom she didn't have in London. She and Bertram spent endless hours wandering the countryside. They studied rocks, insects,

> *"It is all the same, drawing, painting, modeling, the irresistible desire to copy any beautiful object which strikes the eye. Why cannot one be content to look at it? I cannot rest, I must draw, however poor the result."*

and plants. Beatrix watched the animals' behavior closely. Years later, she would put these details in her books.

Potter began working professionally as an artist in 1890, when she created a series of greeting cards. She was quite surprised when they sold well. A few years later, she turned the story she had told her sick young friend into a book. In 1902, *The Tale of Peter Rabbit* was published. In the next ten years, she wrote twenty more books about Peter and his friends.

Potter illustrated all of her books herself, drawing on her lifelong love of nature. Her animal characters, such as Jemima Puddle-Duck, Squirrel

---

WHEN POTTER WAS FIFTEEN, SHE BEGAN KEEPING A DIARY, WHICH SHE WROTE IN A SECRET CODE. NO ONE CRACKED THE CODE UNTIL FIFTEEN YEARS AFTER HER DEATH.

THE TALE OF PETER RABBIT

BY
BEATRIX POTTER
THE ORIGINAL AND AUTHORIZED EDITION
F. WARNE & Cº

A Selected Bibliography of Potter's Work

The Tale of Pigling Bland (1913)
The Tale of Mr. Tod (1912)
The Tale of Jemima Puddle-Duck (1908)
The Pie and the Patty-Pan (1905)
The Tale of Mrs. Tiggy-Winkle (1905)
The Tale of Two Bad Mice (1904)
The Tailor of Gloucester (1903)
The Tale of Squirrel Nutkin (1903)
The Tale of Peter Rabbit (1902)

Nutkin, and Samuel Whiskers, are drawn very accurately—except they wear clothes.

When *The Tale of Peter Rabbit* was published, Potter was thirty-six years old and still living with her parents. By the following year, *Peter Rabbit* had sold 50,000 copies. Using the money from the book sales, Potter bought some land in the Lake District called Hill Top Farm. Potter loved Hill Top Farm and set seven of her books there.

In 1909, while buying another farm in the area, Potter

"Thank goodness I was never sent to school; it would have rubbed off some of the originality."

met a lawyer named William Heelis. Her parents did not think Heelis was good enough for their daughter, but the two married anyway.

By this time, Potter had become less interested in writing and more interested in farming. Although she loved drawing creatures for children, she was happiest spending time with real farm animals.

Potter died on December 22, 1943. She left more than 4,000 acres in the Lake District to the National Trust. This organization preserves the land so that others can enjoy its beauty as much as Potter did.

❧

WHERE TO FIND OUT MORE ABOUT BEATRIX POTTER

BOOKS

Buchan, Elizabeth. *Beatrix Potter: The Story of the Creator of Peter Rabbit.* New York: Frederick Warne, 1998.

Denyer, Susan. *At Home with Beatrix Potter: The Creator of Peter Rabbit.* New York: Harry N. Abrams, 2000.

Wallner, Alexandra. *Beatrix Potter.* New York: Holiday House, 1995.

WEB SITES

BEATRIX POTTER
http://www.ortakales.com/illustrators/Potter.html
To read an extensive biography of Beatrix Potter

THE PETER RABBIT OFFICIAL WEB SITE
http://www.peterrabbit.co.uk/
To read all about Beatrix Potter's most famous character, Peter Rabbit

---

POTTER OWNED A HERD OF RARE HERDWICK SHEEP. SHE WON MANY PRIZES FOR HER SHEEP, AND IN 1930 SHE BECAME THE FIRST WOMAN ELECTED PRESIDENT OF THE HERDWICK SHEEPBREEDERS' ASSOCIATION.

Jack Prelutsky

Born: September 8, 1940

s a young boy, Jack Prelutsky was like many kids. He did not like poetry. He thought it was boring. When he became an adult, Prelutsky realized that poetry could be fun and interesting

for children. He began writing poetry books for children and has become a popular author of children's books. His best-known books of poetry for children include *It's Raining Pigs and Noodles: Poems; A Pizza the Size of the Sun: Poems; The New Kid on the Block: Poems;* and *The Baby Uggs Are Hatching.*

Jack Prelutsky was born on September 8, 1940, in Brooklyn, New York. He attended public schools in New York City. He was not really interested in school and was not a good student. Jack was a challenge for his parents and teachers.

MANY OF PRELUTSKY'S BOOKS OF POETRY HAVE BEEN
ADAPTED AND RECORDED ON CASSETTES.

As a boy, Jack had a beautiful singing voice. When he was ten years old, he was hired to sing at weddings and other events. He was busy almost every weekend because so many people wanted him to sing. A professional opera musician gave Jack free voice lessons. Everyone thought that he would become an opera singer some day.

Jack went to a special arts high school in New York. He was training to be a singer. After he finished high school, Prelutsky attended college for a short time. He listened to professional opera singers and realized that he was not as talented as they were. Prelutsky decided he needed to find another career.

A Selected Bibliography of Prelutsky's Work

Good Sports (2007)
Behold the Bold Umbrelaphant: And Other Poems (2006)
If Not For the Cat (2004)
The Frogs Wore Red Suspenders (2002)
Scranimals (2002)
Awful Ogre's Awful Day (2000)
It's Raining Pigs and Noodles: Poems (2000)
Dog Days: Rhymes around the Year (1999)
Monday's Troll (1996)
A Pizza the Size of the Sun: Poems (1996)
The Dragons Are Singing Tonight (1993)
Something Big Has Been Here (1990)
Tyrannosaurus Was a Beast: Dinosaur Poems (1988)
Ride a Purple Pelican (1986)
It's Snowing! It's Snowing! (1984)
The New Kid on the Block: Poems (1984)
What I Did Last Summer (1984)
The Baby Uggs Are Hatching (1982)
The Headless Horseman Rides Tonight: More Poems to Trouble Your Sleep (1980)
Rolling Harvey Down the Hill (1980)
Circus (1974)

Prelutsky took many jobs to earn a living. In his spare time, he would draw and sketch. He used his imagination to create crazy creatures. One day he decided to write poems to go along with his sketches. He took

"I have always enjoyed playing with words, but I had no idea that I would be a writer. There was a time when I couldn't stand poetry! In grade school, I had a teacher who left me with the impression that poetry was the literary equivalent of liver. I was told that it was good for me, but I wasn't convinced."

them to magazine and book editors to try to get them published. He found an editor who wanted to publish his poems, but who thought his drawings were terrible. The editor told Prelutsky that he should focus on poetry instead of drawing. The editor decided to publish his poetry and still works with Prelutsky today.

Prelutsky's first book was published in 1967. His poems almost always include humor. Prelutsky uses poetry to help kids deal with real issues. He has written poems about dealing with a bully, going to school, and being afraid of the dark.

Prelutsky has been writing poetry for children for more than thirty years. He has published more than forty books for children. He lives in

PRELUTSKY IS FRIENDS WITH BOB DYLAN, THE FOLK AND ROCK MUSICIAN. DYLAN PERFORMED AT A CAFÉ WHERE PRELUTSKY WORKED IN THE 1960S.

the state of Washington with his wife and many pets. Prelutsky spends much of his time traveling around the United States reading poems to children. He also plays the guitar and sings his poems.

❧

WHERE TO FIND OUT MORE ABOUT JACK PRELUTSKY

BOOKS

Berger, Laura Standley, ed. *Twentieth-Century Children's Writers.*
4th ed. Detroit: St. James Press, 1995.

Kovacs, Deborah, and James Preller. *Meet the Authors and Illustrators: 60 Creators of Favorite Children's Books Talk about Their Work.* Vol. 2. New York: Scholastic, 1993.

McElmeel, Sharron L. *100 Most Popular Children's Authors: Biographical Sketches and Bibliographies.* Englewood, Colo.: Libraries Unlimited, 1999.

Potts, Cheryl. *Poetry Fun by the Ton with Jack Prelutsky.*
Fort Atkinson, Wis.: Alleyside Press, 1995.

WEB SITES

THE ACADEMY OF AMERICAN POETS
http://www.poets.org/poet.php.prmPID/68
To read a biography of Jack Prelutksy

SCHOLASTIC
http://teacher.scholastic.com/writewit/poetry/jack_home.htm
To write poetry with Jack Prelutsky

TIME FOR KIDS
http://www.timeforkids.com/specials/story/0,6079,55787,00.html
To read an interview with Jack Prelutsky

———

BEFORE HE BECAME A WRITER, PRELUTSKY ALSO WORKED AS A CAB DRIVER, A BUSBOY, AN ACTOR, A PHOTOGRAPHER, A FURNITURE MOVER, A POTTER, A SCULPTOR, A WAITER, A CARPENTER, A CLERK, A BOOKSELLER, AND A DOOR-TO-DOOR SALESMAN.

Marjorie Priceman

Born: January 8, 1958

Marjorie Priceman's award-winning books are fun. She uses bright watercolors and free-flowing lines to create playful and humorous pictures. Not only is she a talented illustrator, she is also an accomplished author. Priceman illustrates her own stories, as well as the work of other writers.

Marjorie Priceman was born on January 8, 1958, on Long Island, New York. She grew up there in a home filled with books and artwork. Her father loved to read, and her mother was an artist. Marjorie began drawing at an early age. For some strange reason, she liked drawing people from the feet up! In her early

---

IN COLLEGE, PRICEMAN TOOK CLASSES IN DRAWING, PAINTING, METALSMITHING, AND GRAPHICS.

teens, she tried her hand at writing and filmmaking but never finished either project.

After Marjorie graduated from high school, she attended the Rhode Island School of Design, where she studied illustration. After completing her studies, she worked at a variety of jobs in and around New York City. She worked as an illustrator for *Newsday,* a Long Island–based daily newspaper. She also did fashion sketches for several companies and fabric designs for the GapKids clothing stores. But none of these jobs satisfied her.

In the late 1980s, Priceman put her talents to work on a children's book. With the help of a professor at the Rhode Island School of Design, she wrote and illustrated her first book, *Friend or Frog.* It was published in 1989 and chosen as one of ten Top Picture Books of the Year by *Redbook* magazine. The story, about a girl and her frog, is based on Priceman's own family experiences with frogs.

> *"Creating a picture book is like making a movie. . . . Like a screenwriter, you write the story. Like a casting agent, you decide if a character will be played by a short man or a large dog. Like a cinematographer, you choose the camera angles. . . . Like a director, you give directions to the actors. . . . You create your own unique world between the covers of the book."*

PRICEMAN BASED THE ANIMALS IN THE BOOK *ZIN! ZIN! ZIN! A VIOLIN* ON HER OWN ADORABLE CATS.

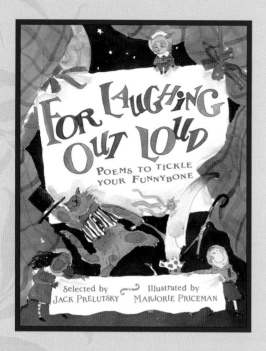

A Selected Bibliography of Priceman's Work

Hot Air: The (Mostly) True Story of the First Hot-Air Balloon Ride (2005)

Princess Picky (2002)

Little Red Riding Hood (2001)

Things That Sometimes Happen (Illustrations only, 2001)

Brand New Kid (Illustrations only, 2000)

Froggie Went A-Courting (2000)

Emeline at the Circus (1999)

My Nine Lives, by Clio (1998)

One of Each (Illustrations only, 1997)

What Zeesie Saw on Delancey Street (Illustrations only, 1996)

Zin! Zin! Zin! A Violin (Illustrations only, 1995)

How to Make an Apple Pie and See the World (1994)

A Nonny Mouse Writes Again!: Poems (Illustrations only, 1993)

For Laughing Out Loud: Poems to Tickle Your Funnybone (Illustrations only, 1991)

Rachel Fister's Blister (Illustrations only, 1990)

Friend or Frog (1989)

Priceman's Major Literary Awards

2006 Caldecott Honor Book
   Hot Air: The (Mostly) True Story of the First Hot-Air Balloon Ride

1996 Caldecott Honor Book
   Zin! Zin! Zin! A Violin

Since the publication of *Friend or Frog*, Priceman has illustrated more than twenty books. She has worked on several poetry books by Jack Prelutsky and picture books by Lloyd Moss. Two of the books Priceman has illustrated have been Caldecott Honor Books.

All of the books Priceman has written and illustrated are popular. *How to Make an Apple Pie and See the World* takes readers around the world to gather ingredients for an apple pie. In *My Nine Lives, by Clio*, children see history through the

"Writing and illustrating books is about the best job imaginable."

eyes of a cat. In the book *Emeline at the Circus,* readers walk into the exciting circus world.

Whether Priceman is illustrating a book about a frog, a violin, or an apple pie, she does it in her own unique style. And she does it with flare. Priceman has made a place for herself in the world of children's books. Her lively illustrations and delightful stories will be charming readers for years to come.

❧

WHERE TO FIND OUT MORE ABOUT MARJORIE PRICEMAN

BOOKS

Rockman, Connie C., ed. *Eighth Book of Junior Authors and Illustrators.*
New York: H. W. Wilson Company, 2000.

Something about the Author. Vol. 81.
Detroit: Gale Research, 1995.

WEB SITES

THE BULLETIN OF THE CENTER FOR CHILDREN'S BOOKS
http://alexia.lis.uiuc.edu/puboff/bccb/0799rise.html
To read an outline about Marjorie Priceman

HALL KIDS ILLUSTRATORS
http://hallkidsillustrators.com/P/18.shtml
To look at a list of books by Marjorie Priceman with links to summaries

STORYBOOKART.COM
http://www.storybookart.com/meet_mpriceman.html
To read a brief biography and samples of Marjorie Priceman's work

———

PRICEMAN WROTE AND ILLUSTRATED TWO BOOKS ABOUT FROGS:
FRIEND OR FROG AND *FROGGIE WENT A-COURTING.*

Laurence Pringle

Born: November 26, 1935

aurence Pringle has always loved the outdoors. Since childhood, he has been interested in nature, animals, and science. He combined his love of writing with these interests. Pringle is the author of many nonfiction books for children and young people.

Most of his books are about science topics. His best-known books include *Death Is Natural; Cockroaches: Here, There, and Everywhere;* and *Energy: Power for People.*

Laurence Pringle was born on November 26, 1935, in Rochester, New York. He grew up in a rural area near Rochester. As a young boy, Laurence spent hours exploring the outdoors.

PRINGLE WRITES ARTICLES FOR CHILDREN'S MAGAZINES. HE SOMETIMES WRITES UNDER THE NAME SEAN EDMUND.

When he was twelve years old, Laurence received a camera as a Christmas present. He brought the camera with him when he went exploring in the forest and took many pictures of birds, flowers, and other things.

A few years later, Laurence began keeping a journal. He wrote about the things that he saw in the forests. When he was about sixteen years old, he wrote an article about crows and sold it to a magazine. This helped Laurence to become more interested in writing.

"My books tend to encourage readers to feel a kinship with other living things, and a sense of membership in the earth ecosystem."

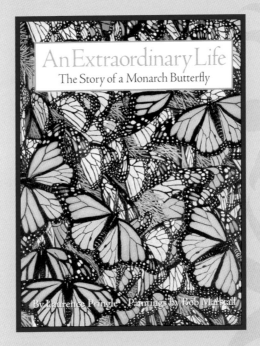

A Selected Bibliography of Pringle's Work

Penguins! Strange and Wonderful (2006)

American Slave, American Hero: York of the Lewis and Clark Expedition (2005)

Come to the Ocean's Edge: A Natural Cycle Book (2003)

Dragon in the Sky: The Story of a Green Darner Dragonfly (2001)

The Environmental Movement: From Its Roots to the Challenges of a New Century (2000)

An Extraordinary Life: The Story of a Monarch Butterfly (1997)

Dolphin Man: Exploring the World of Dolphins (1995)

Coral Reefs: Earth's Undersea Treasures (1995)

The Animal Rights Controversy (1989)

Home: How Animals Find Comfort and Safety (1987)

Here Come the Killer Bees (1986)

Feral: Tame Animals Gone Wild (1983)

What Shall We Do With the Land? Choices for America (1981)

Death Is Natural (1977)

Energy: Power for People (1975)

Follow a Fisher (1973)

Cockroaches: Here, There, and Everywhere (1971)

Dinosaurs and Their World (1968)

Pringle's Major Literary Awards

1998 Orbis Pictus Award
   An Extraordinary Life: The Story of a Monarch Butterfly

1996 Orbis Pictus Honor Book
   Dolphin Man: Exploring the World of Dolphins

"*To do science is to acknowledge that the world is a complex place but that the complexity can be explored and understood, and that there is order and unity in its diversity.*"

Pringle's interest in nature photography has continued throughout his life. Pringle has illustrated some of his books with his own photographs.

After he finished high school, Pringle decided to study wildlife biology. He received two degrees in biology. He also studied journalism.

After college, Pringle took a job as a high-school science teacher. He worked as a teacher for two years. Pringle then became the editor of a science magazine for children.

At the same time, he began writing books about nature and science for children. His first book, *Dinosaurs and Their World,* was published in 1968. After the magazine he worked for went out of business in 1970, Pringle decided to become a full-time writer. He concentrated his efforts on creating nonfiction books about science. Since then, he has written more than ninety books on a variety of science topics.

Pringle believes that science is an important topic for young people. He uses his books to share information about science, writing in a way that makes science interesting for young people. "Children's

AS A YOUNG BOY, LAURENCE PRINGLE BECAME INTERESTED IN BIRD-WATCHING. HE IDENTIFIED BIRDS AND LOCATED THEIR NESTS.

books have a vital role to play," Pringle notes. "They can make science and the universe more accessible to young people."

Pringle continues to write nonfiction books for children and young people. He also presents programs for students on writing and science topics. He lives in West Nyack, New York.

❧

WHERE TO FIND OUT MORE ABOUT LAURENCE PRINGLE

BOOKS

De Montreville, Doris, and Elizabeth D. Crawford, eds. *Fourth Book of Junior Authors & Illustrators.* New York: H. W. Wilson Company, 1978.

Pendergast, Sara, and Tom Pendergast, eds. *St. James Guide to Children's Writers.* 5th ed. Detroit: St. James Press, 1999.

Something about the Author. Autobiography Series. Vol. 6. Detroit: Gale Research, 1988.

WEB SITES

AUTHORS AND ILLUSTRATORS
http://www.authorsillustrators.com/pringle/pringle.htm
For a complete list of Laurence Pringle's works

LAURENCE PRINGLE HOME PAGE
http://laurencepringle.com/
To read about the author and his works

MEET THE AUTHORS AND ILLUSTRATORS
http://www.childrenslit.com/f_pringle.html
To read an interview with Laurence Pringle

———

ALONG WITH MANY AWARDS FOR HIS BOOKS, PRINGLE RECEIVED THE SPECIAL CONSERVATION AWARD IN 1978 FROM THE NATIONAL WILDLIFE FEDERATION.

Alice Provensen
Martin Provensen

Born: August 14, 1918 (Alice)
Born: July 10, 1916   Died: March 27, 1987 (Martin)

The Provensens seemed destined to meet. Both were born in Chicago, Illinois. Both liked books and art and going to watch stunt pilots and air shows. Both came from families that had to move every few years because of the Great Depression, and both settled in California when they were about twelve. Both won scholarships to the School of the Art Institute of Chicago but transferred to the University of California. In later years, they thought about the many times their paths must have crossed. They wondered if they had ever seen each other as children—perhaps sitting across from each other in a public library.

A VISIT TO WILLIAM BLAKE'S INN: POEMS FOR INNOCENT AND EXPERIENCED TRAVELERS WAS A CALDECOTT HONOR BOOK FOR THE PROVENSENS AND WON NANCY WILLARD, THE AUTHOR, A NEWBERY MEDAL. IT WAS THE FIRST BOOK TO WIN BOTH AWARDS.

Alice Provensen was born on August 14, 1918, in Chicago, Illinois. Martin Provensen was born on July 10, 1916, also in Chicago. They didn't meet until the 1940s, though. Alice was working as an animator at Walter Lantz, the studio that made the Woody Woodpecker cartoons. Martin was working at the Walt Disney Studio making character sketches for films like *Fantasia* and *Dumbo.* Then World War II (1939–1945) came. Martin joined the navy, which assigned him to work on animated training films—at Lantz. Martin and Alice finally met.

> *"In any kind of work there is a great sense of support in having someone beside you whose skill and judgment you trust. It is true of bookmaking. There are so many decisions to be made—the page size, the choice of type, the paper, and the fitting of the pictures to the text."*
> —the Provensens

The two married in 1944, and a year later they moved to New York to work as illustrators. They bought a farmhouse north of the city and set up their studio in the barn. The first book they illustrated was *The Fireside Book of Folksongs,* which was published in 1947. They went on to work together as illustrators or writer-illustrators on more than forty books. The list includes *The Golden Bible for Children: The New Testament; My Little Hen; Karen's Curiosity; Shaker Lane; A Visit to William Blake's Inn: Poems for Innocent and Experienced Travelers;* and many more.

———

MOST OF THE ANIMALS IN THE PROVENSENS' ILLUSTRATIONS LIVED ON THEIR FARM—EXCEPT FOR COWS. THEY BORROWED THOSE FROM NEIGHBORS WHEN THEY NEEDED THEM.

A Selected Bibliography of the Provensens' Work

Klondike Gold (2005)

Day in the Life of Murphy (2003)

The Animal Fair (1999)

The Buck Stops Here: The Presidents of the United States (1990)

Shaker Lane (1987)

Town & Country (1984)

The Glorious Flight: Across the Channel with Louis Blériot, July 25, 1909 (1983)

A Visit to William Blake's Inn: Poems for Innocent and Experienced Travelers (Illustrations only, 1981)

The Golden Serpent (Illustrations only, 1980)

A House and a Hound, a Goat and a Gander (1979)

The Year at Maple Hill Farm (1978)

Our Animal Friends at Maple Hill Farm (1974)

My Little Hen (1973)

Roses Are Red. Are Violets Blue? A First Book about Color (1973)

The Provensen Book of Fairy Tales (1971)

Who's in the Egg? (1970)

Tales from the Ballet (1968)

Aesop's Fables (Illustrations only, 1965)

Karen's Curiosity (1963)

The Golden Bible for Children: The New Testament (Illustrations only, 1953)

A Child's Garden of Verses (Illustrations only, 1951)

The Fuzzy Duckling (Illustrations only, 1949)

The Fireside Book of Folksongs (Illustrations only, 1947)

THE GLORIOUS FLIGHT
ACROSS THE CHANNEL WITH LOUIS BLÉRIOT
BY ALICE AND MARTIN PROVENSEN

The Provensens' Major Literary Awards

1984 Caldecott Medal
   The Glorious Flight: Across the Channel with Louis Blériot, July 25, 1909

1982 Boston Globe-Horn Book Picture Book Award
1982 Caldecott Honor Book
   A Visit to William Blake's Inn: Poems for Innocent and Experienced Travelers

The Provensens believed in complete collaboration. Leonard Marcus, an expert on children's literature, said that it wasn't possible to tell who did what on their books. Alice told him they learned to collaborate by being animators. "If you weren't satisfied with a drawing and didn't know what to do next," Alice says, "the other person could help you along. Of course, it had to be the right person, one who understood what you were trying for."

The Provensens both loved airplanes. Near their home, was an airfield with a famous collection of World War I (1914–1918) planes, and Martin took lessons and learned to fly. Eventually, they decided to do a book on a pilot named Louis

Blériot. In 1909, he became the first person to fly across the English Channel. *The Glorious Flight: Across the Channel with Louis Blériot, July 25, 1909,* was published in 1983 and won the Caldecott Medal.

Martin Provensen died at the age of seventy on March 27, 1987. Alice Provensen wasn't sure at first that she wanted to continue illustrating. But then, inspired by the sign that President Harry Truman used to keep on his desk, she wrote and illustrated *The Buck Stops Here: The Presidents of the United States.* A long partnership may have ended, but the work continues.

> *"We were a true collaboration. Martin and I really were one artist."*
> —Alice Provensen

◈

WHERE TO FIND OUT MORE ABOUT ALICE PROVENSEN AND MARTIN PROVENSEN

BOOKS

Marcus, Leonard S. *Side by Side.* New York: Walker & Co., 2001.

Rockman, Connie C., ed. *The Ninth Book of Junior Authors and Illustrators.* New York: H. W. Wilson Company, 2004.

WEB SITES

ALICE PROVENSEN GALLERY
http://www.rmichelson.com/Artist_Pages/Provensen/Alice_Provensen_Gallery.html
To see illustrations by Alice Provensen

HALL KIDS ILLUSTRATORS
http://hallkidsillustrators.com/P/19.shtml
To get a list of books by Alice and Martin Provensen with links to summaries

———

MARTIN AND ALICE PROVENSEN WERE SUPPOSED TO DO THE ORIGINAL ILLUSTRATION FOR TONY THE TIGER, OF KELLOGG'S FROSTED FLAKES FAME. THEY WERE TOO BUSY, THOUGH, AND ANOTHER ARTIST TOOK THE ASSIGNMENT.

Philip Pullman

Born: October 19, 1946

Whether he is transporting readers back in time to Victorian England or to some faraway fantasy world, Philip Pullman is a storyteller without compare. A native of England, Pullman is celebrated on two continents. His fiction books for children and young adults are popular with people of all ages in both Great Britain and the United States. Pullman is perhaps best known for the series His Dark

Materials. This award-winning three-book fantasy series has brought Pullman fame and fortune.

Philip Pullman was born on October 19, 1946, in Norwich, England. Philip's father and stepfather were both Royal Air Force fliers. Philip spent his early years traveling throughout the world with his mother and brother. As a

---

PULLMAN HAS SOLD THE SCREEN RIGHTS TO THE HIS DARK MATERIALS SERIES. FANS CAN LOOK FORWARD TO SEEING HIS NOVELS MADE INTO MOVIES.

boy, Philip visited Africa, Australia, and many other exotic places. These strange and wonderful new lands sparked Philip's imagination and had a lasting effect on him.

Because they were constantly moving, Philip and his brother relied on each other for company and friendship. Together, the two of them made up fantastic games of make-believe, complete with stories about spaceships, castles, and battles. This was Philip's first introduction into the world of imagination.

When Philip was eleven, his family settled down in northern

> " 'Thou shalt not' is soon forgotten, but 'Once upon a time' lasts forever."

A Selected Bibliography of Pullman's Work

Aladdin and the Enchanted Lamp (2005)
The Scarecrow and His Servant (2005)
Lyra's Oxford (2003)
Puss in Boots: The Adventures of That Most Enterprising Feline (2001)
The Amber Spyglass (2000)
I Was a Rat! (2000)
Clockwork, or, All Wound Up (1998)
Detective Stories (1998)
The Subtle Knife (1997)
The Fireworkmaker's Daughter (1995)
The Golden Compass (1995)
The Tin Princess (1994)
The White Mercedes (1993)
The Broken Bridge (1992)
Spring-Heeled Jack (1991)
The Tiger in the Well (1990)
Shadow in the North (1988)
The Ruby in the Smoke (1987)
Count Karlstein (1982)

Pullman's Major Literary Awards

1995 Carnegie Medal
The Golden Compass

Wales in Great Britain. At school, he gained a reputation as an artistic type, a boy who preferred reading, music, and the arts. After he graduated from college, Pullman became a middle-school teacher. His favorite subjects to teach were mythology, storytelling, and literature. Pullman loved nothing better than to fascinate his students by weaving wild and wonderful tales.

Eventually, Pullman left his teaching job and began writing full time. Over the years, he has won a number of important awards and honors for his writings. He received the Carnegie Medal for *The Golden Compass,* the first book in the series His Dark Materials. The Carnegie Medal is the top prize given in Great Britain for children's literature. In 2001, Pullman became the first children's book author to win the Whitbread Award, one of the oldest and most distinguished literary awards in Great Britain. Pullman won the award for *The Amber Spyglass,* the last book in His Dark Materials.

> *"We don't need lists of rights and wrongs, tables of do's and don'ts: We need books, time, and silence."*

Pullman lives in Oxford, England. He says that his wife, Judith, and his two sons are his best critics. For years, Pullman has worked in a shed in his garden. Inside the shed are two comfortable chairs, hundreds of books, a six-foot-long stuffed rat, and assorted other items to spark

WHEN BRITISH BOOKS ARE PUBLISHED IN THE UNITED STATES, THEIR TITLES SOMETIMES CHANGE. THE FIRST BOOK IN PULLMAN'S HIS DARK MATERIALS SERIES IS CALLED *THE GOLDEN COMPASS* IN THE UNITED STATES AND *NORTHERN LIGHTS* IN ENGLAND.

his imagination. There is also a computer in the shed, although Pullman prefers to write his books by hand first.

Each day, Pullman tries to complete three pages of writing. He starts work in the morning, taking a break in the afternoon for lunch and a television show. Once a week, Pullman spends the day answering his fan mail.

"Stories are the most important thing in the world. Without stories, we wouldn't be human beings at all."

Fans of Pullman's work can expect more spellbinding stories in the future. Pullman says he loves writing and expects to continue doing it for the rest of his life.

WHERE TO FIND OUT MORE ABOUT PHILIP PULLMAN

BOOK
Authors and Artists for Young Adults. Vol. 15. Detroit: Gale Research, 1995.

WEB SITES
PHILIP PULLMAN HOME PAGE
http://www.philip-pullman.com
For information about Philip Pullman and his works

POWELLS BOOKS
http://www.powells.com/authors/pullman.html
To read an interview with Philip Pullman

RANDOM HOUSE
http://www.randomhouse.com/features/pullman/philippullman/
To read about Philip Pullman

SOME OF PULLMAN'S BOOKS ARE BASED ON PLAYS HE WROTE FOR STUDENTS WHEN HE WAS A TEACHER. ONE SUCH BOOK IS *THE RUBY IN THE SMOKE,* FEATURING SASSY TEEN HEROINE SALLY LOCKHART.

Chris Raschka

Born: March 6, 1959

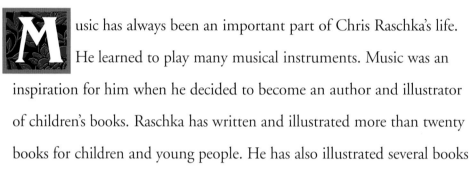

Music has always been an important part of Chris Raschka's life. He learned to play many musical instruments. Music was an inspiration for him when he decided to become an author and illustrator of children's books. Raschka has written and illustrated more than twenty books for children and young people. He has also illustrated several books

written by other authors. His best-known books include *Charlie Parker Played Be Bop, Arlene Sardine, Yo! Yes?* and the Thingy Thing series.

Chris Raschka was born on March 6, 1959, in Huntington, Pennsylvania. His mother was from Austria, and Chris spent his early years growing up in Germany. Chris's parents met while they were working in Europe after World War II (1939–1945). He attended first grade in a German school and learned how to speak both

IN *YO! YES?* RASCHKA USES ONLY THIRTY-FOUR WORDS THROUGHOUT THE ENTIRE BOOK TO TELL HIS STORY OF MAKING FRIENDS.

English and German. His family moved back to the United States a few years later. The rest of Chris's childhood was spent in Chicago.

Chris loved both music and art as a child. He began taking piano lessons when he was six years old. He also learned how to play the recorder and the viola. He played in orchestras in high school and college.

Chris was also interested in animals. "I just loved animals of all types, especially crocodiles and turtles," Raschka says. "I also loved drawing and music, but never thought I could make a living at those."

> *"My books are my own thoughts about things that are important to me. I work through how I feel about such things as language, art, music, and friendship with these loose, colorful, and slightly wild drawings."*

Raschka decided to study biology in college. When he finished college, he planned to work on a crocodile farm in India. Instead, he took a job at a children's clinic in Germany. He enjoyed working with children at the clinic, and he decided that he wanted to go to medical school and become a doctor.

Before he was supposed to start medical school, Raschka went to the Virgin Islands with his wife, Lydie. The two decided to work on their art there. Raschka was successful, and some of his work was displayed in art galleries. He also was hired to work as an illustrator.

EVEN AFTER HIS FIRST BOOK WAS PUBLISHED, RASCHKA CONTINUED TO PURSUE HIS LOVE OF MUSIC. HE PLAYED THE VIOLA IN TWO PROFESSIONAL SYMPHONY ORCHESTRAS. HOWEVER, HE STOPPED PLAYING THE VIOLA BECAUSE OF PAIN IN HIS HAND.

A Selected Bibliography of Raschka's Work

Five For a Little One (2006)

The Hello, Goodbye Window (2005)

Kick in the Head (2005)

Boy Meets Girl; Girl Meets Boy (Illustrations only, 2004)

Talk to Me About the Alphabet (2003)

Be Boy Buzz (2002)

Little Tree (Illustrations only, 2001)

Waffle (2001)

Doggy Dog (2000)

Fishing in the Air (Illustrations only, 2000)

Goosey Goose (2000)

Lamby Lamb (2000)

Moosey Moose (2000)

Ring! Yo? (2000)

Whaley Whale (2000)

Wormy Worm (2000)

Another Important Book (Illustrations only, 1999)

Happy to Be Nappy (Illustrations only, 1999)

Like Likes Like (1999)

Arlene Sardine (1998)

Mysterious Thelonious (1997)

Simple Gifts: A Shaker Hymn (Illustrations only, 1997)

The Blushful Hippopotamus (1996)

The Genie in the Jar (Illustrations only, 1996)

Can't Sleep (1995)

Elizabeth Imagined an Iceberg (1994)

Yo! Yes? (1993)

Charlie Parker Played Be Bop (1992)

The Owl and the Tuba (Illustrations only, 1991)

R and R: A Story about Two Alphabets (1990)

Raschka's Major Literary Awards

1994 Caldecott Honor Book
  Yo! Yes?

2006 Caldecott Medal
2005 Boston Globe-Horn Book Picture Book Honor Book
  The Hello, Goodbye Window

Soon, Raschka and his wife returned to the United States. On the night before his first class for medical school was supposed to begin, he decided not to go. Instead, he found work in Michigan as an illustrator for newspapers and magazines.

After a couple of years as an illustrator, Raschka decided to try to create a children's book. He moved to New York City in 1989. His first book, *R and R:*

"My goal is to create a book where the entire book—text, pictures, shape of book—work together to create the theme. The placement of images and text on the page is crucial for me."

A Story about Two Alphabets, was published in 1990. His other books for children include stories about jazz musicians.

Raschka lives with his wife in New York City. He continues to write and illustrate books for children and young people.

❧

WHERE TO FIND OUT MORE ABOUT CHRIS RASCHKA

BOOKS

Holtze, Sally Holmes, ed. *Seventh Book of Junior Authors & Illustrators.* New York: H. W. Wilson Company, 1996.

Something about the Author. Vol. 80. Detroit: Gale Research, 1995.

WEB SITES

CHILDREN'S LITERATURE
http://www.childrenslit.com/f_raschka.html
To read an article about Chris Raschka

FIRST PERSON BOOK PAGE
http://www.bookpage.com/9809bp/chris_raschka.html
For an interview with Chris Raschka

HORN BOOK
http://www.hbook.com/publications/magazine/articles/mar98_raschka.asp
To read words from Chris Raschka

NOVELLO FEATURED GUEST
http://www.novellofestival.net/archiveguest.asp?id=25
For a biography of Chris Raschka

———

RASCHKA WROTE *CHARLIE PARKER PLAYED BE BOP* TO THE RHYTHM OF A JAZZ TUNE. THE BOOK IS WRITTEN MORE LIKE A SONG THAN A STORY.

INDEX